a SAVOR THE SOUTH® *cookbook*

Catfish

SAVOR THE SOUTH® *cookbooks*

Catfish, by Paul and Angela Knipple (2015)
Shrimp, by Jay Pierce (2015)
Gumbo, by Dale Curry (2015)
Sweet Potatoes, by April McGreger (2014)
Southern Holidays, by Debbie Moose (2014)
Okra, by Virginia Willis (2014)
Pickles and Preserves, by Andrea Weigl (2014)
Bourbon, by Kathleen Purvis (2013)
Biscuits, by Belinda Ellis (2013)
Tomatoes, by Miriam Rubin (2013)
Peaches, by Kelly Alexander (2013)
Pecans, by Kathleen Purvis (2012)
Buttermilk, by Debbie Moose (2012)

a SAVOR THE SOUTH® *cookbook*

Catfish

PAUL AND ANGELA KNIPPLE

The University of North Carolina Press CHAPEL HILL

© 2015 Paul and Angela Knipple
All rights reserved. Manufactured in the United States of America.
SAVOR THE SOUTH® is a registered trademark of the
University of North Carolina Press, Inc.
Designed by Kimberly Bryant and set in Miller and
Calluna Sans types by Rebecca Evans.

The paper in this book meets the guidelines for permanence and durability of the Committee on Production Guidelines for Book Longevity of the Council on Library Resources. The University of North Carolina Press has been a member of the Green Press Initiative since 2003.

Jacket illustration: depositphotos.com/©ajafoto

Library of Congress Cataloging-in-Publication Data
Knipple, Paul.
Catfish / by Paul and Angela Knipple.
pages cm. — (Savor the south cookbooks)
Includes index.
ISBN 978-1-4696-2130-2 (cloth : alk. paper)
ISBN 978-1-4696-2131-9 (ebook)
1. Cooking (Catfish) 2. Cooking, American—Southern style.
I. Knipple, Angela. II. Title.
TX748.C36K56 2015   641.6'92—dc23
2014024702

19 18 17 16 15   5 4 3 2 1

*We dedicate this book to
fidgety grandchildren and patient grandparents,
to cane poles and bait of all sorts.
No matter what you catch, you have set a hook
firmly in good memories.*

Contents

INTRODUCTION Zen and the Art of Catfishing 1

Fried Catfish 16
THE BASICS

Thin-Fried Catfish 18
Fried Whole Catfish 20
Fried Catfish Steaks 22
Popcorn Catfish 24
Fried Catfish Fillets 26
Tartar Sauce 27
Coleslaw 28
Hushpuppies 29
Pickled Green Tomatoes 30
White Beans 32
Cajun Cabbage 33

Appetizers 35

Catfish and Bacon Brochettes 36
Catfish with Baba Ghanoush 38
Catfish Croquetas 40
Catfish Empanadas 42
Dodson Lake Samosas 45
Coriander Catfish Rolls 48

Catfish Fritters 50

Mississippi Bao 51

Smoky Catfish Mousse 54

Smoky Catfish Brandade Spread 56

Tea-Smoked Catfish 58

Soups and Stews 61

Catfish Chowder 62

Catfish Gumbo 64

Catfish-Rice Soup with Ginger and Onion 66

Nigerian Catfish Stew 68

Indonesian Spicy-and-Sour Catfish Soup 70

Szechuan Catfish Stew 72

Catfish Sauce Piquant 74

Salads and Sandwiches 77

Creamy Catfish-Pecan Salad 78

Grilled Catfish Salad 80

Catfish Po'Boys 82

Catfish Burgers 84

Catfish Tacos 86

Catfish *Bánh Mì* 88

Entrées 91

Baked Catfish with Citrus 92

Butter-Poached-Catfish Surf and Turf 94

Maple Planked Catfish 96

Blackened Catfish 98

Jerk Catfish 100

Colombian Catfish Pie 102

Catfish *en Papillote* 104

Delta Paella 106

Mediterranean-Style Steamed Catfish 108

Hungarian-Style Catfish Paprika with Sour Cream Noodles 110

Moroccan Catfish Tagine 112

Catfish and Vegetable Tempura 114

Miso-Marinated Catfish 116

Caramelized Clay Pot Catfish 118

Thai Green Catfish Curry 120

Catfish 61 122

Nashville-Style Hot Fried Catfish 124

Noodled Catfish Casserole 126

Beer-Battered Catfish and Chips 129

Catfish Pudding 132

Cross-Eyed Catfish with Wavy Gravy 134

Acknowledgments 137   *Index* 139

a SAVOR THE SOUTH® *cookbook*

Catfish

Introduction

ZEN AND THE ART OF CATFISHING

For southerners, catfish is about more than the meal. There's also the hunt. Giant catfish were always the topic of stories about "the one that got away."

We were no different. When we were growing up in and around Memphis, our fishing trips were adventures that only children can have and, perhaps, that can be experienced only with grandparents leading the way.

Angela's catfish history begins with an almost-forgotten southern creation—rag bologna. You may have seen it behind small-town deli counters or hiding in the lunchmeat section. It was labeled "imitation bologna," which begs the question, "Really? Imitation bologna? Isn't bologna one of those things you like to eat but try not to think about what's in it, kind of like hot dogs?"

Well, it turns out that rag bologna is a cousin of the slugburger. What in the world is a slugburger, and isn't this book supposed to be about catfish? Back during the Great Depression, when our grandparents were growing up, people used fillers like soy meal, bread crumbs, or flour to stretch ground meat. In North Mississippi, the slugburger, a combination of beef and soy meal, was born. Another more common meat containing a filler throughout the region was rag bologna, slightly sweeter and less spicy than the real thing and wrapped in, you guessed it, rags.

Here's where catfish come into the story. Angela's grandfather swore by rag bologna as catfish bait. His fishing ritual began with breakfast at the country store, where he and his friends from decades back would share stories and swap news. That's also where he and Angela bought their rag bologna bait, packed up lunch, and got a couple of icy cold sodas and Angela got to pick a toy off the less-than-a-dollar rack. Plastic dinosaurs were a favorite, but army men would do in a pinch. Then it was off to the lake.

To call this a lake is an exaggeration. It's a big pond that anchored the community where they lived. Angela was taught that fishing meant tying a hook on a cane pole, baiting it with rag bologna, throwing the line in the water, setting the pole in the bank, and waiting. You had to be still, or the fish would see your shadow move and stay away. You had to be quiet, or they'd hear you and go deep. You couldn't expect them to bite right away; catfish have to have time to inspect the bait and decide whether they want it. If you didn't catch any that day, it wasn't a failure; it just wasn't meant to be. You would still look upon it as a day well spent. Zen and the art of catfishing.

They usually caught some fish, but the ritual of the day and the time spent together were most important. There were, however, rules. If you caught a fish, you had to decide its fate immediately—free it or clean it. Angela learned to clean fish early and remembers being squeamish about eating the first fish she cleaned, but that's part of the experience too.

Paul's story is similar. When he was around six, his grandmother took him to visit her brother. When they arrived, Uncle Lee was just about to go out onto the pond behind his house to check his trotlines.

A trotline is a line tied between two trees, poles, or other stationary objects over a body of water. Other lines are tied to it, hooked, baited, and left to dangle in the water. The idea is that, rather than spending the day waiting on the bank, the fisherman can set the lines, go about his business, and then return later to "trot" along the bank retrieving the catch. This is a results-oriented system, not a relax-on-the-bank-with-a-pole system.

Being too small to go out on the boat, Paul was left to watch, sorely disappointed, from the bank as Uncle Lee and his own grandson hauled in a forty-seven-pound monster. Among Paul's family mementos is a picture of him and his cousin with Uncle Lee, who is holding a fish that Paul remembers, not entirely incorrectly, being nearly as long as he was tall.

For Paul's family, one fished for more than just the thrill. Another of Paul's distinct catfish memories involves his grandmother's brother-in-law, Uncle Henry, who was at the center of one of

Paul's earliest food memories, a memory that's integral to Paul's connection to food.

On one visit, Uncle Henry had just returned from fishing at one of his two ponds, and Paul got his first lesson in putting meat on the table by dispatching a living creature and preparing it for consumption. Paul cleans catfish today using the very same methods. This experience impressed on Paul not only the fragility of life but also the importance of the tools in Uncle Henry's tackle box. This wasn't a spectacle for Paul's benefit. It was life and death—a way of life and life itself.

This is not to say that a day with catfish turned a young boy into a philosopher and a young girl into a Zen master. It simply shows how our personal food histories began with catfish.

Catfish on the Plate

The steamy sweet white meat of catfish encased in golden crisp cornmeal was a part of childhood for both of us. It was there at church suppers and fundraisers, at family reunions and family suppers.

For Angela, catfish is the taste of coming home. There's a catfish restaurant near the Memphis airport called Catfish Cabin. She used to travel a great deal for work, and after returning to the Memphis airport, it was always her first stop for a massive glass of sweet tea and a plate of crispy fish. For Paul, it's one of the first restaurants he can remember going to, digging into a plate of fish with perfect hushpuppies filled with crisp corn kernels and a touch of heat from jalapeños. We don't hesitate to take anyone there when we pick them up at the airport. It's a catfish indoctrination.

No two catfish restaurants are alike. They run the gamut from private fish camps and one-room shacks poised on riverbanks to inland palaces of piscine glory. In some, the history is focused on the men who bring the catch to the table, while in others, the history of the region or the fish takes pride of place. You may ask how different one piece of fried catfish can really be from another, and if you ever set out on a fried catfish quest, you'll be amazed at the variety that abounds. Secret spice mixtures are as important to catfish restaurants as they are to barbecue joints.

Catfish is often served as part of the classic "meat and three" plate all over the South, but just as often it's served on its own, especially in areas where the fish swim in local rivers or ponds. You'll find yourself ordering at a counter or giving your order to a congenial waitress at your table. You'll sit where you like or be escorted to a table you reserved in advance. The atmosphere can range from homey to rustic, with a smattering of high cotton and romance mixed in to let you know that catfish doesn't have to be a simple dish these days.

While the iconic catfish meal puts fried fillets on a plate, you're just as likely to find those fillets in a sandwich or po'boy. You'll find catfish in traditional stews all over the South. You'll find it smoked and grilled and blackened. And now you're not unlikely to sit down in a fine-dining restaurant to a thick pan-sautéed fillet served with a rich beurre blanc.

Why Catfish?

Southerners almost take for granted the special status they've bestowed on catfish; it's tied irrevocably to our DNA. Perhaps it's because the catfish evokes such visceral memories for many of us. Perhaps it's because fried catfish has been the centerpiece of family gatherings or church picnics, events that are gems of childhood memories.

Native Americans were enjoying the catfish of southern rivers long before European explorers even thought about setting sail across the Atlantic. We like to think, though, that catfish were part of nature's bounty that Native Americans shared willingly with the first settlers who struggled to find sources of nourishment in their new home. One thing we know for certain is that both European and African American settlers preferred to bread their catfish with cornmeal flavored with seasonings and fry it to keep it moist.

Since catfish has a long history as a southern food, it makes sense that it has become a major dish in our foodways. It's easily available since it's common in our lakes and rivers. It's not hard to catch because it's not a picky eater. It's economical: bait is cheap, and aside from an initial outlay for equipment, all fishing costs is time. If you have to buy it, it's cheap. It stretches: a large catfish can make dinner for a family, and the ingredients for a fish fry are inexpensive and likely to be on hand in any southern pantry. And, of course, it just tastes good.

But aren't there other fish in the South? Of course there are. There are restaurants devoted to serving the bream and crappie caught in Reelfoot Lake in Tennessee, and there's no denying the popularity of bass and trout as both game fish and food fish. But no fish is as common across the region as catfish, and no fish has captured our imaginations or embedded itself so thoroughly in our culture as has the humble, bewhiskered catfish.

Catfish and Popular Culture

Like us, much of the South loves catfish. In fact, we would go so far as to say that the catfish is the king of southern fish. Consider the range of its empire. The catfish capital of the world is Belzoni, Mississippi. And Savannah, Tennessee. And Des Allemands, Louisiana. West Tawakoni is only the catfish capital of Texas, but given the size of Texas, that's no small achievement.

Catfish has pushed each of these cities into the limelight because of its popularity as a food and catfishing's popularity as a sport. A large portion of the catfish on America's tables is farmed within sixty miles of Belzoni. The catfish eaten in the Savannah area is all wild-caught from the Tennessee River; restaurants selling catfish from the river dot its banks. The catfish around Des Allemands is wild-caught in the bayous; in Northeast Louisiana, the catfish is farmed. In West Tawakoni, the catfish industry isn't about getting the fish on the plate but about getting it in the boat. Sports fishing for catfish is a large part of the tourism industry and culture in East Texas.

Whether catfish is a livelihood or a lifestyle, it's a cause for celebration. Each of these "capitals" hosts a catfish festival, a fishing tournament, or both. Des Allemands hosts the Louisiana Catfish

Festival. The first annual festival took place in 1975, and that year Louisiana governor Edwin Edwards proclaimed the town the Catfish Capital of the World. In 1980, the state legislature apparently decided a promotion was in order and passed a resolution declaring Des Allemands the Catfish Capital of the Universe.

Like its Louisiana neighbor, Belzoni throws a festival with an emphasis on good eats and good times. There's no shortage of fun, and for those up to the challenge, there's a catfish-eating contest. Since Savannah is on a river, its annual festival is a bit different. With the area's emphasis on wild-caught catfish, it includes the six-week-long National Catfish Derby, featuring a world championship catfish cook-off, catfish-skinning competition, and fishing competition. West Tawakoni hosts the first event of each year's national catfish tournament season.

Other cities get in on the fun as well. Paris, Tennessee, hosts the world's biggest fish fry, serving over five tons of fried catfish to thousands of catfish lovers every year. Elgin, South Carolina, is home to the Catfish Stomp, featuring fried catfish and the star of the Stomp, catfish stew. Morgantown, Kentucky, hosts the Green River Catfish Festival. Franklin Parish in Northeast Louisiana and the town of Washington in the south of the state host festivals, but it's Conroe, Texas, that holds the Cajun Catfish Festival. Kingsland, Georgia; Crescent City, Florida; and Ware Shoals, South Carolina, have festivals; Ware Shoals actually calls its event a "feastival." And the list goes on.

The reach of the South's beloved bewhiskered fish extends into popular culture, even sports. In Detroit, octopi are traditionally thrown onto the ice during Red Wings hockey games as a good luck charm. In Nashville, fans of the city's hockey team, the Predators, have taken up the tradition with a southern flair, and catfish find their way onto the ice.

From 2003 to 2008, the Columbus Catfish played Class A minor-league baseball in Columbus, Georgia. Though the Catfish are no more, the Carolina Mudcats now play in Zebulon, North Carolina. North Carolina baseball icon James Hunter was given the nickname "Catfish" by Charles O. Finley, the owner of the first major-league team he played for, because Finley felt Hunter needed a catchy nickname. Now "Catfish" Hunter is immortalized in the Baseball Hall of Fame.

The catfish has its place in music as well. Indeed, "Catfish" Hunter was himself the subject of two songs. In 1975, Bob Dylan wrote "Catfish" about the pitcher. Joe Cocker and Kinky Friedman both covered the song. Bobby Hollowell, a friend of Hunter in his youth, wrote "The Catfish Kid (Ballad of Jim Hunter)," which was recorded in 1976 by Big Tom White.

Bluesman Robert Petway wrote and recorded "Catfish Blues" in 1941. Although he recorded very few songs, his lyrics were influential, especially the second verse: "Well if I were a catfish, Mama / swimming deep down in the deep blue sea. / All these gals now / setting out hooks for me." Muddy Waters adapted the tune and lyrics for his 1950 hit "Rollin' Stone," including the first verse: "Well, I wish I was a catfish, / swimmin' in a oh, deep, blue sea. / I would have all you good lookin' women, / fishin', fishin' after me." The popularity of Waters's song inspired a group of young English fellows looking for a name for their band—the Rolling Stones.

Another English band, Jethro Tull, released the rock album *Catfish Rising* in 1991. In 1976, the Four Tops released an album titled *Catfish*, featuring a song of the same name. Among the songs of the hard-driving Jethro Tull and the soulful Four Tops and countless other songs and albums about catfish, the most elegant musical tribute to catfish is in George Gershwin's opera *Porgy and Bess*. Set on Catfish Row in Charleston, a fictionalized version of the actual Cabbage Row, Gershwin's opera is based on the novel and play *Porgy* by DuBose Heyward. Although the lyrics are considered racist by some, the opera is universally considered to be a masterpiece.

Other novels, stories, and poems feature catfish, including Mark Twain's great American novel, *The Adventures of Huckleberry Finn*. As Huck and Jim float down the Mississippi River, they fish for their food: "About the first thing we done was to bait one of the big hooks with a skinned rabbit and set it and catch a cat-fish that was as big as a man, being six foot two inches long, and weighed over two hundred pounds. . . . He would a been worth a good deal over at the village. They peddle out such a fish as that by the pound in the market house there; everybody buys some of him; his meat's as white as snow and makes a good fry."

A World of Catfish

Catfish are an extremely diverse species that reach far beyond the South, having existed at one time or another along the coasts or in the rivers of every continent on Earth except Antarctica (and they may even be there hiding under the ice). Wherever they are, they wend their way into the imaginations of the people who live around them.

Zuni folklore tells of a father who promised to give a catfish the first thing he saw on returning home in exchange for wealth for his family. He expected to see his dog but instead saw his youngest son, who ended up being raised by the catfish under the water.

In Japan, earthquakes were blamed on restless catfish or *namazu*. The thrashing of these massive fish was said to be the cause of the earth shaking. Popular art from the Edo earthquake of 1855 is particularly striking, with imagery of huge kimono-clad catfish sipping tea with the rich and those who would profit from repairing the damage caused by the earthquake.

The enormous seventeen-foot-long Wels catfish of northern Europe is a stock character of horror folklore. While the fish have been seen to eat small mammals, there have been no confirmed reports of one ever eating a human.

Whether small enough to fit in a fish bowl or a ten-foot-long monster of the Mekong River region of Southeast Asia, catfish are everywhere. But most of the varieties eaten all over the world are medium sized, the same size you'll find in grocery stores and catfish farms here in the United States. Because the catfish is so geographically diverse and such a good source of nutrition, catfish are featured in traditional recipes from all corners of the globe. We share some of our favorites with you here.

Not everyone sings the praises of the catfish, however. Nearly two centuries ago, in 1837, one Captain Marryat of the Royal

Navy called the Mississippi River "the great common sewer of the Western America." He also noted that "it contains the coarsest and most uneatable of fish, such as the cat-fish and such genus."

In 1883, Mark Twain came to the defense of the river and the catfish. In *Life on the Mississippi*, where Marryat is quoted, Twain wrote: "As a panorama of emotions sent weltering through this noted visitor's breast by the aspect and traditions of the 'great common sewer,' it has a value. A value, though marred in the matter of statistics by inaccuracies; for the catfish is a plenty good enough fish for anybody."

Even in this millennium, the catfish has its critics. Some cooking shows decry the "muddy taste" of catfish. Modern farmed catfish and wild-caught catfish from clean water don't taste muddy. In stagnant water, catfish can take on strong flavors from the algae through their skin or gills. For people who grew up eating catfish caught from stagnant ponds, that's just how catfish tastes. To them, farm-raised catfish is "missing something."

Bringing Catfish to the Shore and the Table

The channel catfish—the fish we tried to catch as children, a native of the warm waters of the southeastern United States and the most common species for fishing and eating—is a natural bottom dweller. Living in almost total darkness at the bottoms of lakes and rivers, channel catfish find food using taste buds in their skin and the eight catlike "whiskers" around their mouths.

The blue catfish is larger and more common in the faster-flowing rivers and deep reservoirs of the South. While not as commonly farmed as the channel catfish, the blue catfish is the most popular game fish of the species. Like the channel catfish, the blue catfish will eat live prey, but it also eats almost any organic matter it finds. Urban legend erroneously claims that its muddy flavor comes from the fish's diet.

Another reason for catfish's reputation for bad flavor comes from a popular type of catfish bait called stinkbait. Exactly what it sounds like, stinkbait is dead fish or shrimp or some other malodorous material that can be attached to a hook. In the catfish's dark world, giving it a hint where the bait is gives fishermen an advantage.

Commercial fish-farming operations avoid the problem of muddy flavor by raising fish in ponds where the water is circulated to maintain the proper oxygen level. The movement of the water minimizes the risk of algae growth, and the water quality is monitored constantly. In the days leading up to the fish harvest, fish are tested for flavor. If any strong flavors are present, the fish aren't harvested until the water quality improves and the flavor of the fish is clean. Better flavor is just one benefit of fish farming; U.S. farmed catfish has been named a "Best Choice" for sustainability by the Monterey Bay Aquarium Seafood Watch program.

Despite the quality and eco-friendliness of farmed catfish, the fishing industry is under threat on multiple fronts. The first is an influx of lower-priced imported fish, primarily from Vietnam. In 2003, imports made up 3 percent of catfish sales. By 2009, that number had increased to 57 percent. U.S. fishermen have begun to fight back, citing health concerns rather than unfair trading practices. The farm bill passed in 2008 required the USDA to inspect imported fish, but the agency hasn't yet begun to enforce the new rules. Some states are taking matters into their own hands. In 2009, after tests in state labs on imported catfish revealed FDA-banned antibiotics, Alabama banned the importation of catfish from five Asian countries.

Another threat to the industry comes from within the United States. The price of corn is directly tied to the production of catfish in two ways. First, the high cost of corn as a feed ingredient makes farming the fish less profitable. Second, the profitability of corn—especially given the greatly reduced labor that raising it requires in comparison to raising catfish—leads some catfish farmers to fill in their ponds to plant row crops.

Still, having catfish on the table is a growing tradition in the South. For many southerners, catfish is the first fish they remember eating. Restaurants across the South still proudly serve U.S. catfish. In an interview with CBS News, Alabama restaurant owner Debbie Brown said local residents would "run me out of town" if she served foreign catfish.

Tradition isn't the only thing keeping catfish on southern tables, though. With the growth of the local food movement and the resurgence of farmers' markets, catfish farmers have found a new, more profitable market in direct consumer sales. And even with price competition from imported fish, domestic catfish still offers an exceptional bargain when compared to most other fish in the grocery store, particularly when its low environmental impact is taken into consideration.

A Few Notes on Buying and Preparing Catfish

When selecting catfish, make sure you're buying American farm-raised catfish. If there's no sign stating where the fish is from, it's probably not American. If you're buying catfish at a seafood counter, ask for American catfish. You'll be surprised how much difference it makes when retailers know their customers want local fish.

Catfish, like any other fish, shouldn't have a "fishy" odor. The flesh should be firm. The flesh of steaks and whole catfish should adhere firmly to the bone. Feel free to ask your fishmonger questions. You want to get the freshest fish possible. Take your purchased fish home promptly and keep it cold. Ideally, use it within twenty-four hours.

To preserve quality in frozen fish, each piece of American farm-raised catfish is individually quick frozen. The IQF process means that the fish will be just as fresh when you thaw it as when it was harvested. If you purchase frozen catfish, thaw it in the refrigerator when you're ready to prepare it. Lay out pieces in a single layer in a nonreactive container and cover them to prevent them from picking up flavors in the refrigerator. Allow them to thaw completely before preparing them. To thaw frozen fish more quickly, place the container of fish in a cold water bath. Don't allow the water to enter the fish container. Never thaw fish directly in water; the fish will lose its firm texture.

Catfish is a firm, quick-cooking fish. It's generally done in 10 minutes or less, making it perfect for frying. In other dishes that require more time for flavors to develop and other ingredients to cook, catfish can be added near the end of cooking. The flaky white fish also takes on the flavors of marinades well.

Catfish generally comes in one of four cuts:

* "Whole" catfish are technically catfish that are "headed, eviscerated, and skinned," as defined by the Catfish Institute. But at every place we've ever eaten catfish, this cut is called whole fish on the menu, even though there are no eyes looking back at you from the plate.
* Catfish steaks are made by cutting 1-inch cross sections of the fish. Each steak has two meaty medallions at the top and two thinner slivers of meat at the bottom. These morsels are divided by a cross-shaped set of bones, centering on the spine. Steaks cut from the tail end of a fish will be oval-shaped. Steaks from the head end will be horseshoe-shaped because of the cavity of the fish.
* Fillets have become the catfish cut of choice. For a family with children, the lack of bones is the biggest plus. For restaurants and for most of the recipes in this book, fillets allow the most flexibility. The diner doesn't want a full meal? Make him or her a sandwich with a single fillet. Or get fancy and offer blackened, crab-stuffed, étouffée, or smothered catfish fillets. We encourage you to experiment with all forms of catfish, but having fillets on hand isn't a bad idea, and you can get them in sizes to suit any appetite. Fillets classified as small weigh 3–5 ounces. Large fillets weigh 7–9 ounces. As with any other fish, you should always check fillets for bones by running your fingertips over the surface. Bones do get through on rare occasions; remove them with your fingernails or a clean pair of tweezers.
* Catfish nuggets are the result of the catfish industry's effort to not waste any of the meat of the fish. They can also be a low-cost ingredient for any catfish dish that requires the fish to be cut into pieces. While fillets are taken from the sides

of the fish and are regularly shaped, nuggets are taken from the belly of the fish and are irregular. Nuggets work perfectly for soups and stews, in which expensive fillets would have to be cut up. Just be aware that nuggets sometimes have bits of bone and a thin membrane that you'll need to remove. While this membrane is edible, if you trim it away with a sharp, thin-bladed knife, no one will know you didn't use fillets and you'll save money.

About Deep-Frying

Since deep-frying is one of the most common ways to cook catfish, this book begins with a chapter on fried catfish. Don't let deep-frying intimidate you. With the proper equipment and a little know-how, you can make a tasty batch of fried catfish quickly and safely.

EQUIPMENT

For frying, the first consideration is your pot. Dedicated fryers come with everything you need to monitor the temperature, add and remove food, and prevent oil splatter. Fryers are less versatile, though, than a good heavy pot, which you can use to cook a roast in the oven or catfish stew on the stove.

To choose a good deep fryer, look for one with a digital thermometer that's easy to read. You don't want to have to lean over a fryer full of hot oil to read the tiny numbers. You also want one with a basket large enough to cook the amount needed to feed your family. If you need to feed six people and the fryer only holds two fillets, it's not the one for you. Make sure you understand how the oil drains from the fryer before you get it home. You need to be able to drain it without help from someone else.

If you decide to purchase a pot instead of a deep fryer, look for a heavy one, preferably cast-iron, to best maintain a constant temperature. The pot should be at least 5 inches deep to ensure that the oil doesn't boil over.

If you plan to use a pot, you'll also need to buy a few other things. You'll need an oil thermometer to maintain the correct temperature. Like the thermometer on a deep fryer, it should be easy to read. Also, a splatter screen makes cleanup easier.

A large mesh strainer spoon known as a spider is the best tool to use with deep-fried foods. It doesn't damage delicate batter the way tongs might when you're turning food, and it lets the oil drain away when you lift food from the pot.

OIL

We recommend using peanut or soy oil for deep-frying because of the neutral flavor and high smoke point of those oils, meaning they can be raised to high temperatures without risk of burning. While deep-frying is never healthy, peanut oil is a relatively healthy choice that's both economical and easy to find. For those with peanut allergies, soy oil is a good choice.

Oil can be used more than once. After it has cooled, filter it through a mesh sieve lined with coffee filters or paper towels. Oil lasts longest when stored in the freezer, but even at room temperature, a sealed container of used oil will last for months; just smell it for rancidity before using it. Don't use oil that's dark or frothy. Never use oil that has fried savory food to fry sweet food and vice versa, and oil that has fried fish should only be used for frying fish or hushpuppies.

Finally, be sure to dispose of cooking oil properly. Pour cool, used oil into a nonbreakable container. Some cities allow you to donate your used cooking oil to be turned into biodiesel. Other cities ask that you simply throw the oil away with the rest of your trash.

SAFETY

Deep-frying safety consists of a few simple rules. First, before you begin to heat the oil, make sure your pot or fryer is stable and placed where you can reach it easily. Moving a pot of hot oil is very dangerous. If an oil fire should start on your stove, put it out with a kitchen fire extinguisher. If you don't have a fire extinguisher, put a lid on the pot or throw baking soda or salt on the fire to extinguish it. Never pour water on an oil fire. The water will only spread the oil and make the fire worse.

Don't drop food into the oil. Slide it in slowly or lower it on a spoon or other utensil. Dropping food into hot oil can cause it to splatter. Foods with a high moisture content will splatter. Never pour liquid into hot oil. Use hot pads or mitts when handling the pot and cooking utensils. Don't overheat the oil. In addition to burning food, oil that's too hot begins to break down and can add bad flavors to food; it can also catch fire. At no time should you leave oil unattended on the stovetop or in the fryer. If you must leave the room, turn off the heat and remove the pot from the burner. And never leave children unsupervised around hot oil. Finally, when you're done cooking, allow adequate time for the oil to cool.

HOW-TO

If you're using a deep fryer, follow the manufacturer's instructions for determining the proper amount of oil and the desired temperature. If you're deep-frying on the stovetop, bring at least 3 inches of oil to the desired temperature over medium heat. You don't want to use high heat because the temperature will increase too fast and be hard to control once it reaches the target temperature. You don't want to use too little oil because the oil should cover the food you're cooking and there should be room to turn the food in the oil without it touching the bottom of the pan.

Don't try to deep-fry extremely thick pieces of food because the outside will burn before the inside is done. You want the food to have a golden brown exterior. And remember, food will continue to cook briefly after you remove it from the oil.

Whether you're cooking on the stovetop or in a deep fryer, always let the oil return to the proper temperature between batches to maintain consistent results.

Fried Catfish
THE BASICS

The two keys to frying catfish, aside from using good-quality catfish and fresh oil, are using the right breading and determining the correct frying temperature. Breading can vary in thickness as a result of minor changes in the process. The best temperature for frying ranges from 325° to 375°, depending on the thickness of the catfish; a lower temperature is best for thicker pieces because it allows the meat to cook through without burning the breading.

All of the breadings in these recipes contain cornmeal. We've found that finely ground cornmeal, sometimes sold as masa, but not masa harina, provides the best coating and texture for some recipes. You can find masa in most supermarkets, although it's typically made from white corn. It's fine to use white masa, but the freshly ground yellow-corn masa offered by some small mills throughout the South and beyond is even better. If you can't find masa, don't worry. Regular cornmeal will work just fine. Just keep in mind that the coarser the grind, the heartier the crunch.

Catfish is served at meat-and-three restaurants across the South, so it comes with many different sides.

The sides included here are mostly those found at the typical catfish shack. Feel free to serve your fried catfish with any sides you want, but for an authentic experience, serve plenty of sweet tea or lemonade with it and you'll have everything you need.

Thin-Fried Catfish

John T. Edge wrote an article in Garden & Gun *magazine titled "100 Southern Foods You Absolutely, Positively Must Eat before You Die." Naturally he included fried catfish, but what's interesting is that he divided it into two categories: thick-fried and thin-fried. Thick-fried is what we normally think of as fried catfish, although his recommendation of Taylor Grocery in Taylor, Mississippi, for its sublime thick-fried is spot-on.*

Thin-fried is a far more unusual beast. A signature of Middendorf's Restaurant in Manchac, Louisiana, the dish is more like chips than fish fillets—the exterior is perfectly crisp, and the interior has just a hint of moistness and sweet catfish flavor. Middendorf's recipe is a closely guarded secret. This is a decent approximation, but as with all great dishes, there's sure to be at least one thing we just didn't know about.

While the instructions are straightforward, this is the most difficult recipe in this book. Cutting a catfish fillet into perfect thin fillets is difficult. At Middendorf's, thin-fried catfish comes out looking like huge flower petals practically floating on the plate. The first time you make this, you'll appreciate the skill it requires. It takes lots of practice, and even then you might end up with smaller pieces than you had hoped for. The key is to cut pieces that are relatively even in thickness so they cook consistently. Aim for small thin pieces rather than large lumpy ones. Don't overthink it. If the cuts don't turn out perfect the first time, you'll still have tasty catfish. And there will always be a next time.

MAKES 2 SERVINGS

4 large catfish fillets (about 2 pounds)
1 cup cornmeal, preferably stone-ground
1¼ teaspoons salt
½ teaspoon freshly ground black pepper
½ teaspoon cayenne pepper

Heat at least 3 inches of soy or peanut oil to 350° in a deep pot or deep fryer.

Preheat the oven to 200°. Place a wire rack over a baking sheet.

Rinse the fillets and pat them dry. Check for and remove any bones.

Lay a fillet flat on a cutting board with the pointy end facing you. Using a sharp, thin knife like a boning knife, cut about 1 inch off the thick end of the fillet. This will give you a flat surface to start cutting into. Place the blade of the knife parallel to the cutting board against the flat surface of the fillet at the thick end, about ¼ inch below the top. Lay your hand flat on top of the fillet to hold it in place. Gently slice horizontally into the fillet, using long smooth strokes and being careful not to cut upward into your hand, to create thin fillets. If your cuts are uneven, trim the individual pieces to smooth them out into thinner, flatter pieces. Repeat with the remaining fillets.

In a large bowl, combine the cornmeal, salt, black pepper, and cayenne pepper, whisking to distribute the seasonings evenly.

Dredge the fillets in the cornmeal mixture one at a time, coating them evenly on both sides. Gently shake off any excess.

Working in batches, fry the fillets for 1–2 minutes, or until golden brown and crisp. Place the fillets on a paper towel–lined plate to drain. Transfer the fillets to the prepared baking sheet and place them in the oven to keep warm. Be sure the oil has returned to 350° before frying the next batch.

Fried Whole Catfish

Many people prefer catfish fillets so they don't have to deal with the bones, but the bones are a big part of the experience. We believe that, as with any cut of meat cooked on the bone, the bones of the catfish add flavor during cooking. What's more, whole catfish provide one of the most sublime tastes you'll ever experience. The fin along the belly of the catfish holds a tiny bite of fatty sweet meat that rivals the finest tuna. Just be careful when sucking the meat off the small bones of the fin.

Dredging the fish in buttermilk adds a thin layer to hold the masa. Using masa instead of cornmeal creates a very light and smooth breading.

MAKES 2 SERVINGS

- 1 cup buttermilk
- ½ teaspoon hot sauce
- 1 cup masa
- 1¼ teaspoons salt
- ½ teaspoon freshly ground black pepper
- ½ teaspoon cayenne pepper
- 4 whole catfish (about 2 pounds)

Heat at least 3 inches of soy or peanut oil to 325° in a deep pot or deep fryer.

Preheat the oven to 200°. Place a wire rack over a baking sheet.

Whisk together the buttermilk and hot sauce in a wide, shallow dish.

Combine the masa, salt, black pepper, and cayenne pepper in another wide, shallow dish, whisking to distribute the seasonings evenly.

Rinse the fish and pat them dry, both on the outside and inside the cavity.

Dredge a fish in the buttermilk mixture, coating both the outside and the inside and lifting the fins to make sure they're coated as well. Shake off any excess. Dredge the fish in the masa mixture, coating it evenly inside and out and making sure the fins are coated as well. Repeat with the remaining fish.

Working in batches, most likely one fish at a time, fry the fish for 6–7 minutes, or until golden brown and cooked through to the bone. Place the fish on a paper towel–lined plate to drain. Transfer the fish to the prepared baking sheet and place it in the oven to keep warm. Be sure the oil has returned to 325° before frying the next fish.

Fried Catfish Steaks

Catfish steaks aren't as popular in the United States as they once were, perhaps because they're more expensive and they have to come from larger fish. They're also more challenging to eat because of the small segments of bones. Catfish steaks are still available in some stores and through catfish farmers, and you'll still find them in some restaurants, especially those that have been around for a long time. The Pickwick Catfish Farm Restaurant in Counce, Tennessee, is famous for its smoked catfish, but steaks are the star of its fried menu.

The breading for this recipe is the thickest used in this chapter. The fine masa clings to the moist fish and soaks up more buttermilk, which holds more cornmeal.

MAKES 2–4 SERVINGS

- 1 cup masa
- 1¼ teaspoons salt, divided
- 1 cup buttermilk
- ¼ teaspoon hot sauce
- 1 cup cornmeal, preferably stone-ground
- ½ teaspoon freshly ground black pepper
- ½ teaspoon cayenne pepper
- 8 catfish steaks (about 2 pounds)

Heat at least 3 inches of soy or peanut oil to 350° in a deep pot or deep fryer.

Preheat the oven to 200°. Place a wire rack over a baking sheet.

In a medium bowl, combine the masa and ¼ teaspoon of the salt, whisking to distribute the salt evenly.

In a second medium bowl, whisk together the buttermilk and hot sauce.

In a third bowl, combine the cornmeal, the remaining 1 teaspoon salt, the black pepper, and the cayenne pepper, whisking to distribute the seasonings evenly.

Rinse the steaks and pat them dry, trimming off any fin bits or ragged edges.

Dredge a steak in the masa mixture, coating it lightly but evenly on both sides. Dredge the steak in the buttermilk mixture, covering it evenly. Shake off any excess. Dredge the steak in the cornmeal mixture, making sure to create an even coating. Shake off any excess. Repeat with the remaining steaks.

Working in batches, fry the steaks for 3–4 minutes, or until golden brown and crisp. Place the steaks on a paper towel–lined plate to drain. Transfer the steaks to the prepared baking sheet and place them in the oven to keep warm. Be sure the oil has returned to 350° before frying the next batch.

Popcorn Catfish

Popcorn catfish isn't a traditional item at catfish shacks, but while we have the fryer heated up and the cornmeal out, we might as well have fun and make some. It makes a great snack for game day or a movie. The egg and milk mixture combines with the flour and masa to make more of a batter than a breading. The masa contributes the corn flavor and texture that we associate with fried catfish, while the seasonings provide a different flavor.

MAKES 2 SERVINGS

- 1 egg, beaten
- 1 cup milk
- 1 tablespoon Worcestershire sauce
- 1 pound catfish fillets, cut into bite-sized pieces
- ½ cup all-purpose flour
- ½ cup masa
- 1 teaspoon paprika
- 1 teaspoon garlic powder
- ¼ teaspoon cayenne pepper
- Salt

Heat 3 inches of soy or peanut oil to 375° in a deep pot or deep fryer.

In a medium bowl, add the egg, milk, and Worcestershire sauce, stirring to combine. Add the catfish and toss to coat each piece.

Combine the flour, masa, paprika, garlic powder, and cayenne pepper and 1 teaspoon salt in a paper bag or gallon-sized resealable bag. Remove the catfish pieces from the milk mixture with a slotted spoon and place them in the bag. Close the bag tightly and shake it to coat the catfish pieces with the breading.

Working in batches, carefully lower the catfish pieces into the hot oil. Fry, stirring to separate, until the catfish is golden brown and crisp, 2–3 minutes. Place the catfish on a paper towel–lined plate to drain. Sprinkle with salt to taste.

Serve with lemon juice, hot sauce, and tartar sauce.

Fried Catfish Fillets

Of all the ways to serve catfish, there's nothing finer than a simple fried fillet. Crunching in with a fork or, better yet, tearing off a bite with your fingers is a thrill. Sweet steam rising from the flaky white fish is a promise of the delights to follow.

Any cornmeal will work for the breading, but stone-ground cornmeal offers the best corn flavor and crunch.

MAKES 4 SERVINGS

- 8 large or 16 small catfish fillets (3–5 pounds)
- 1 cup cornmeal, preferably stone-ground
- 1¼ teaspoons salt
- ½ teaspoon freshly ground black pepper
- ½ teaspoon cayenne pepper

Heat at least 3 inches of soy or peanut oil to 350° in a deep pot or deep fryer.

Preheat the oven to 200°. Place a wire rack over a baking sheet.

Rinse the fillets and pat them dry. Check for and remove any bones.

In a large bowl, combine the cornmeal, salt, black pepper, and cayenne pepper, whisking to distribute the seasonings evenly.

Dredge the fillets in the cornmeal mixture one at a time, coating them evenly on both sides. Gently shake off any excess.

Working in batches, fry the fillets until golden brown and crisp (5–6 minutes for large fillets, 3–4 minutes for small). Place the fillets on a paper towel–lined plate to drain. Transfer the fillets to the prepared baking sheet and place them in the oven to keep warm. Be sure the oil has returned to 350° before frying the next batch.

Tartar Sauce

Tartar sauce is used on fish other than catfish, and the sauce isn't even an American original, but you won't come across a catfish shack that doesn't serve it. Generally, it's a creamy sauce with chopped ingredients added for texture. The British and the French each have their own variety. In the South, tartar sauce can be as simple as mayonnaise, pickle juice, and minced onion. This recipe is a blend of the best of both American and British traditions.

MAKES 2 ½ CUPS

- 2 cups mayonnaise
- 2 tablespoons lemon juice
- 2 tablespoons minced onions
- 1 tablespoon chopped dill pickles
- 1 tablespoon chopped capers
- 1 tablespoon minced parsley
- ¼ teaspoon sugar (optional)

Combine all ingredients in a medium bowl and mix until well blended.

Coleslaw

In the South, there are two types of coleslaw. The first is barbecue coleslaw. Each of these slaws is as varied as the barbecue it accompanies. The second is catfish coleslaw, which is marked by only the slightest variations from catfish shack to catfish shack. This coleslaw is a slightly sweet mayonnaise-based shredded-cabbage salad. Acceptable additions or substitutions include purple cabbage, sandwich spread, dill or caraway seeds, pickle relish, and more sugar.

MAKES 8 CUPS

- 1 medium head of cabbage
- 1 large carrot, grated
- ¼ cup minced Granny Smith apples
- 2 tablespoons minced red onions
- 1 cup mayonnaise
- ¼ cup sour cream
- ¼ cup sugar
- ¼ cup apple cider vinegar
- ¼ teaspoon celery seeds
- ¼ teaspoon freshly ground black pepper
- ¼ teaspoon salt

Core the cabbage and remove and discard the outer leaves. Shred the cabbage and place in a large bowl. Add the carrot, apples, and red onions, stirring to combine.

In a medium bowl, add the mayonnaise, sour cream, sugar, vinegar, celery seeds, pepper, and salt. Whisk until the sugar is dissolved. Taste and adjust the seasoning.

Pour the dressing over the cabbage mixture and toss to moisten thoroughly. Cover and refrigerate for at least 2 hours. Serve cold.

Hushpuppies

To paraphrase Roy Blount Jr., catfish is easy; hushpuppies are hard. Far too many places serve dense, overcooked, greasy, or flavorless hushpuppies, and it's a downright shame. Hushpuppies should be light, with a fluffy interior and a crispy exterior. This recipe has the right balance of ingredients to achieve that. The egg and buttermilk keep the hushpuppies moist, while the baking powder and baking soda keep them light. The keys to cooking these are to not overcrowd the fryer and to keep them moving so they cook evenly.

MAKES 8 SERVINGS

- ¾ cup stone-ground cornmeal
- ½ cup all-purpose flour
- 1 egg
- 1 cup buttermilk
- ½ cup diced yellow onions
- ½ cup frozen corn kernels
- 1 (4.5-ounce) can chopped green chili peppers (optional)
- ¾ teaspoon baking powder
- ¼ teaspoon baking soda
- 1 teaspoon sugar
- 1 teaspoon salt
- ½ teaspoon freshly ground black pepper

Heat at least 3 inches of soy or peanut oil to 375° in a deep pot or deep fryer.

Combine all ingredients in a large bowl, stirring until well combined.

Carefully drop the batter by spoonfuls into the hot oil, working in batches so as not to overcrowd the fryer. Cook the hushpuppies, turning often, until they're golden brown on all sides, 2–3 minutes. Place on a paper towel–lined plate to drain.

Pickled Green Tomatoes

Catfish is sweet; tartar sauce is creamy. What's needed is some acid to cut through all that. The side of choice isn't a cucumber pickle but a green tomato pickle because the green tomatoes bring extra flavor to the party. You still want some sweetness here, though, to maintain balance. The acid should cut through the richness of the other dishes but not through the roof of your mouth. The amount of sugar may seem like a lot, but give it a try before you reduce it.

MAKES 2 PINTS

- 1 pound green tomatoes, cut into bite-sized pieces
- 2 garlic cloves, minced
- ½ teaspoon brown mustard seeds
- ¼ teaspoon cumin seeds
- ¼ teaspoon dill seeds
- ½ teaspoon red chili flakes
- 1 cup water
- 1 cup white vinegar
- 6 tablespoons sugar
- 1 tablespoon salt

SPECIAL EQUIPMENT
- 2 (1-pint) jars, preferably wide-mouth
- 2 lids with rings

Sterilize the jars and lids by submerging them in boiling water for 5 minutes. Remove the jars and lids and set them upside down on paper towels to dry. They should be cool enough to handle by the time you're ready to use them.

In a large bowl, combine the green tomatoes, garlic, mustard seeds, cumin seeds, dill seeds, and chili flakes. Toss to combine the ingredients. Distribute the mixture evenly between the 2 jars, leaving about ½ inch of headspace.

Bring the water and vinegar to a boil in a small saucepan over medium-high heat. Add the sugar and salt and stir until both have dissolved completely. Carefully pour the boiling vinegar mixture into the jars, leaving ½ inch of headspace. You may not need all of the vinegar mixture.

Cover the jars with the lids and tighten the rings. Allow the pickles to cool to room temperature, then refrigerate for at least 6 hours. The pickles will last in the refrigerator, unopened, for 2 months.

White Beans

As a rule of thumb, catfish shacks aren't high-end operations. Rather than featuring white tablecloths, they represent years of tradition stemming from leaner times. All of the traditional sides are a matter of economy. Slaw? Cabbage is cheap. Pickled green tomatoes? Green tomatoes are pickled and canned so they don't go to waste at the end of summer. Dried beans are probably the cheapest ingredient of all, yet with the right treatment, they're delicious.

This dish doesn't have to accompany catfish. It can be a meal on its own when served with cornbread or hushpuppies. And any beans not eaten right away can be frozen for reheating on a cold day.

MAKES 8–12 SERVINGS

- 1 pound dried white beans, sorted and rinsed
- ½ pound country ham, diced, or 1 country ham shank
- 1 medium yellow onion, diced
- 1 bay leaf
- 1 teaspoon freshly ground black pepper
- Salt

In a large stockpot, cover the beans with water and bring to a boil over medium-high heat. Cook for 2 minutes. Cover the beans, remove them from the heat, and let them rest for at least 1 hour.

Add the country ham, onion, bay leaf, and pepper to the beans, stirring to combine. Simmer the beans over medium-low heat, stirring occasionally, for 2 hours, or until the beans are tender and some are bursting.

If you used a ham shank, remove it from the beans carefully and allow it to cool enough to touch. Remove the meat from the bone, dice it, and return the meat to the beans. Discard the bone. Discard the bay leaf before serving. Season with salt to taste.

Cajun Cabbage

We discovered this dish at Soul Fish Restaurant in Memphis and loved it so much we decided to include our own variation in this book, even though it's not a traditional side dish for catfish. It's perfect even for the anticabbage crowd. The andouille sausage and Cajun seasoning add great flavor, and the cooking time is limited so the stewed cabbage funkiness isn't overwhelming.

MAKES 8 SERVINGS

- 2 slices bacon
- 8 ounces andouille sausage, sliced into thin rounds
- 1 medium yellow onion, diced
- 1 garlic clove, minced
- 1 head cabbage, chopped
- ½ cup water
- 1 teaspoon Cajun seasoning
- ½ teaspoon salt

Heat a skillet over medium-low heat. Add the bacon and cook until the fat is rendered and the bacon is crisp, about 10 minutes. Place the bacon on a paper towel–lined plate to drain, leaving as much of the drippings in the pan as possible. Reserve the bacon for another use.

Increase the heat to medium. Add the andouille and cook, stirring often, until it begins to brown, about 10 minutes. Add the onion and continue cooking, stirring frequently, until the onion is translucent, about 5 minutes longer. Add the garlic and cook for 2 minutes. Add the cabbage and water to the skillet. Cook, covered, until the cabbage softens enough to stir easily, about 10 minutes. Add the Cajun seasoning and salt, stirring to combine. Continue cooking, covered, for 5 minutes, or until the cabbage is as soft as you like it.

Appetizers

When it comes to mealtime, folks can put away a mess o' catfish. When it comes to offering something small to start a meal or a snack to pass around, catfish is light and versatile enough to fill the bill.

This chapter offers up catfish as handheld bites, including catfish on a stick, catfish as a tasty spread for crackers, and catfish as the star of attractive plates of hors d'oeuvres. There's a world of possibilities beyond fried catfish. You'll still break out your fryer, but in this chapter, we help you break out of your shell.

To paraphrase Robert Earl Keen Jr., we're taking catfish where it's never been before, and we're taking you with us.

Catfish and Bacon Brochettes

There's something about an appetizer served on a stick. An appetizer made up of a bunch of good ingredients rolled together and then skewered is even better. Brochette *is the French term for a skewered dish. Other cultures have shish kabobs, satay, and souvlaki. Technically, since this dish is also rolled, it could be called* roulade en brochette, *but we'll just call it tasty.*

MAKES 6–8 SERVINGS

1 stick butter, at room temperature
1 bunch Italian parsley, minced
6 small catfish fillets (about 1½ pounds)
12 slices thin-cut bacon, halved
Salt

SPECIAL EQUIPMENT
Bamboo or small metal skewers

In a small bowl, combine the butter and parsley until the parsley is evenly mixed through. Refrigerate for at least 1 hour before using.

Preheat the oven to 400°.

Slice each catfish fillet in half lengthwise, then crosswise. Generously smear one side of each strip of catfish with the parsley butter.

Lay a half slice of bacon flat. Top the bacon with a strip of catfish. Sprinkle the catfish lightly with salt. The amount of salt you need will vary depending on the saltiness of the bacon you're using. Carefully roll the bacon and catfish lengthwise, keeping the bacon on the outside. Secure the roll with a skewer, piercing completely through it. Repeat with the remaining bacon and catfish.

Prepare a roasting pan with a drip tray. Place the brochettes in a single layer on the roasting pan. Cook for 35–40 minutes, or until the bacon on the outside is crisp and sizzling.

The brochettes can also be cooked on a grill over indirect heat.

Catfish with Baba Ghanoush

Casablanca Restaurant in Memphis offers baba ghanoush with grilled shrimp. The Mediterranean seasoning on the shrimp makes for a spicy sweetness that pairs perfectly with the earthy sweetness of the eggplant and tahini in the baba ghanoush. Because shrimp and farm-raised catfish have a similar firmness and sweetness, we offer this recipe as an homage to our friend Aimer Shtaya, the owner of Casablanca.

MAKES 4 SERVINGS

FOR THE BABA GHANOUSH
- 1 large eggplant
- ¼ cup plain Greek yogurt
- 3 tablespoons lemon juice
- 2 tablespoons tahini
- 1 tablespoon extra-virgin olive oil, plus more for serving
- ½ cup minced Italian parsley
- 1 garlic clove, minced
- ¼ teaspoon cumin
- 1 teaspoon salt
- Paprika

FOR THE CATFISH
- 3 small catfish fillets (about ¾ pound)
- 1 tablespoon extra-virgin olive oil
- ½ teaspoon turmeric
- ½ teaspoon paprika
- ¼ teaspoon ginger
- ¼ teaspoon cumin
- ¼ teaspoon cinnamon
- ½ teaspoon salt
- ¼ teaspoon white pepper
- Pinch of cayenne pepper

TO SERVE
Warm pita bread

To make the baba ghanoush, preheat the oven to 375°. Generously grease a rimmed baking sheet.

Cut the eggplant in half lengthwise. Place the eggplant halves, cut-side down, on the prepared baking sheet. Bake for 45 minutes, or until the eggplant is very soft. Scoop the eggplant pulp into a strainer set over a bowl. Let the eggplant rest for 30 minutes to allow the excess liquid to drain off.

Transfer the eggplant pulp and remaining ingredients except for the paprika to a food processor and blend until smooth. Spread evenly on a plate, leaving room around the edge for the catfish. Drizzle the baba ghanoush with olive oil and sprinkle with paprika.

To make the catfish, heat a medium skillet or grill pan over medium-high heat.

Cut each fillet across the grain into 4 roughly equal pieces. In a medium bowl, pour the oil over the fish and toss with your hands to coat the fish evenly. Add the spices and continue tossing to coat the fish.

Working in batches if necessary, sear the fish in the skillet for 2–3 minutes per side.

To serve, arrange the catfish around the baba ghanoush and serve with warm wedges of pita bread.

Catfish Croquetas

Croquetas are a popular Spanish tapa, a small serving of food intended as a bar snack, appetizer, or part of a series of small courses that make up a meal. In Spain, the most common filling is ham, but catfish works nicely with the subtle flavor of smoked paprika. The base of the croqueta is a bechamel sauce, a roux cooked with milk. This is the sauce that's used as a filling in pot pies, so with the crunchy breading and the moist filling, croquetas are similar to a handheld pot pie. Serve them alone or with a simple sauce of piquillo peppers blended with olive oil until smooth.

Plan ahead when preparing these. Because of the rich creaminess of the filling, the croquetas need to spend some time in the refrigerator to set before and after breading.

MAKES 8 SERVINGS

- 4 tablespoons butter
- 2 tablespoons extra-virgin olive oil
- ½ cup all-purpose flour
- 1½ cups whole milk, heated
- 1¼ teaspoons salt
- ¾ teaspoon smoked paprika
- ½ teaspoon white pepper
- 1 pound catfish fillets, minced
- 3 eggs
- 1½ cups fine breadcrumbs

Heat the butter and olive oil in a medium saucepan over medium heat. Once the butter has melted, add the flour and stir to combine. Continue to stir for 2 minutes, or until the flour is well blended. Stirring constantly, slowly add the heated milk, salt, smoked paprika, and white pepper and continue cooking for 2 minutes. Slowly add the minced catfish, stirring to combine. Continue cooking for 1 minute. Remove from the heat.

Lightly oil a 9 × 13-inch baking dish. Spoon the catfish mixture into the dish and spread evenly. Let the mixture cool to room temperature, cover tightly, and refrigerate for at least 2 hours or up to overnight to allow the mixture to set.

Break the eggs into a small bowl and whisk to blend thoroughly. Place the breadcrumbs in a medium bowl. Line a baking sheet with parchment paper.

Using 2 spoons or your hands, shape the catfish mixture into roughly walnut-sized croquetas. Roll each croqueta in the breadcrumbs, dip it into the eggs, then roll it again in the breadcrumbs, coating it evenly. Lay the breaded croquetas in a single layer on the prepared baking sheet. Repeat until all of the catfish mixture is used, then refrigerate for 30 minutes.

Preheat the oven to 200°. Line a baking sheet with several layers of paper towels.

Heat at least 3 inches of soy or peanut oil to 350° in a deep pot or deep fryer.

Working in batches of no more than 6 at a time, cook the croquetas in the hot oil for 2–3 minutes, or until they're golden brown on all sides, keeping them submerged with a slotted spoon. Use the slotted spoon to remove the croquetas, allowing as much oil to drain off as possible. Transfer them to the prepared baking sheet and keep them warm in the oven. Be sure the oil has returned to 350° before frying the next batch.

Catfish Empanadas

Empanadas are meat-stuffed pastries that are either baked or fried. They're popular in various forms throughout South America, Spain, Portugal, and other places where Spanish and Portuguese colonizers landed. Like tamales, empanadas are a handheld meal, but the thin crust is more delicate and allows for more flavors to mingle in the filling. Empanada dough needs to be soft enough to stretch over the filling but strong enough not to break. To make the dough firm enough to work with, you'll need to refrigerate it while you make the filling.

Once the empanadas have finished baking, serve them with red or green salsa and guacamole.

MAKES 24 EMPANADAS

FOR THE DOUGH
- 4 cups all-purpose flour
- 1 teaspoon salt
- 2/3 cup lard, butter, or both
- 2 eggs
- 1 cup warm milk

FOR THE FILLING
- 2 tablespoons lard or butter
- 1 medium yellow onion, diced
- 1 yellow bell pepper, diced
- Salt
- 1 pound catfish fillets, diced
- 1/2 cup fresh or frozen corn kernels
- 1 tablespoon adobo seasoning
- 1 1/2 teaspoons cumin
- 1/2 teaspoon ancho chili powder
- 1/4 teaspoon cayenne pepper

1 bunch green onions, finely chopped
1 bunch cilantro, finely chopped
1 teaspoon lime juice

TO FINISH
1 egg, separated

To make the dough, combine the flour, salt, and lard or butter in a large bowl, working in the lard with your hands or a pastry cutter until the flour combines with the lard in pieces no larger than rice grains. Add the eggs and milk and gently work the mixture until a soft, clumpy dough forms. Transfer the dough to a lightly floured surface and form a ball. Cover loosely and refrigerate for at least 30 minutes.

To make the filling, melt the lard or butter in a large deep skillet over medium-high heat. Add the onion and bell pepper with a pinch of salt and cook, stirring occasionally, for 10 minutes, or until the onion and bell pepper are soft. Add the catfish, corn, adobo seasoning, cumin, ancho chili powder, and cayenne pepper to the onion mixture, stirring to combine. Continue cooking until the fish begins to brown, about 6 minutes.

Remove the skillet from the heat and allow the filling to cool to room temperature. Add the green onions, cilantro, and lime juice, stirring to mix thoroughly. Add salt to taste.

To make the empanadas, flour a work surface lightly. Roll the dough ⅛ inch thick, sprinkling on more flour as needed to prevent sticking or tearing, and cut out circles 5 inches in diameter. Combine the scraps, roll them out, and continue cutting until all of the dough is used.

Mound 1 heaping tablespoon of the filling in the center of each circle. Brush the edge all the way around with a small pastry brush dipped in egg white. Fold the dough over the filling, pressing to seal the pastry all the way around. Crimp the edges of the empanadas by twisting and folding them delicately toward the filling, pressing gently with your fingers to seal tightly.

In a small bowl, whisk the egg yolk with 2 teaspoons water and lightly brush it on top of each empanada. Refrigerate the prepared empanadas for 30 minutes on parchment paper–lined baking sheets.

Preheat the oven to 425°.

Bake the empanadas for 20 minutes, or until the pastry is golden brown.

Dodson Lake Samosas

As far as we know, there's no place named Dodson Lake. Instead, the name of this recipe is a tribute to some wonderful friends. Tommy and Bonnie Dodson grew the best sweet potatoes we ever ate. Sadly, Tommy died while we were writing this book. Earl Lake is our local catfish farmer. He supplied us with so much more than catfish, telling us about the fish themselves and about running a fish farm.

In the United States, samosas are considered a dish that originated in the Indian subcontinent. However, they have a much older and richer history than that. The dish appears to have been created in the Middle East, where it was called sambosa. *A tenth-century Iranian historian mentions* sanbosags. *By the thirteenth century, the dish had crossed Afghanistan into India, where it took on the name* samosa. *Traditionally, nonvegetarian samosas are made with potatoes and minced meat. For our version, we've added southern flair by substituting sweet potatoes and catfish. Otherwise, the flavors are very true to the original. We like to serve them with tamarind, mango, or mint chutney.*

This recipe is inspired by the increasing number of Indian immigrants in the South. For us, new groups of immigrants mean all manner of cultural opportunities, including new foods. Indian markets are opening all across the South. There you'll find chutneys and more. Garam masala is becoming more popular and can be found in some supermarkets, but you'll find a selection of multiple varieties of this spice blend at most Indian markets. Amchur powder is another unusual Indian ingredient. It's a tart powder made from dried green mangoes. Tamarind paste is also hard to find in mainstream markets. This thick paste adds an earthy sourness that nothing else can. If you don't have access to an Indian market, you can order these ingredients from sources on the Internet.

MAKES 25 SAMOSAS

1 large sweet potato, peeled and cubed
2 tablespoons ghee or vegetable oil
½ teaspoon cumin seeds
1 large yellow onion, diced
1 pound catfish fillets, minced
1 (2-inch) piece ginger, grated
2 garlic cloves, crushed
1 teaspoon garam masala
½ teaspoon amchur powder
1 teaspoon coriander
½ teaspoon ground cardamom
½ teaspoon ground cinnamon
3 dried red chili peppers, crushed, or
    1 teaspoon chili pepper flakes
¾ teaspoon salt
½ teaspoon freshly ground black pepper
½ teaspoon tamarind paste
1 egg
1 package 8-inch-square wonton wrappers (25 wrappers)

Bring a medium saucepan of water to a boil over medium-high heat. Add the sweet potato and boil until tender, about 15 minutes. Drain the sweet potato and mash it.

Heat the ghee in a large skillet over medium heat. Add the cumin seeds and stir constantly for 1 minute, or until the seeds have begun to brown. Add the onion and continue cooking, stirring frequently, until soft, about 5 minutes. Add the catfish, ginger, and garlic to the onion mixture and continue cooking for 3 minutes, or until the fish is cooked through. Stir in the garam masala, amchur powder, coriander, cardamom, cinnamon, chili peppers, salt, and pepper. Add the mashed sweet potatoes and tamarind paste and stir until combined. Cover the mixture and chill in the refrigerator for 1 hour.

Heat 3 inches of soy or peanut oil to 375° in a deep pot or deep fryer.

Prepare an egg wash by whisking together 2 tablespoons of water with the egg in a small bowl. Lay out a wonton wrapper. Fold the wrapper in half to make a rectangle. Lay the rectangle on your cutting board so that the long side is facing you and the folded edge is farthest from you. Fold one side of the rectangle up diagonally from the lower corner to near the center so that what was the side of the rectangle now extends about ½ inch above the top of the rectangle. Now fold the other side diagonally, overlapping the first fold by about ½ inch. You should now have a triangle. Gently pick up the wrapper and open it so that you have a cone-shaped pouch in your hand. Place a heaping tablespoon of filling in the pouch. Fold one of the two long pointy flaps of the pouch over the filling, tucking it down as much as possible. Coat the top of this flap with egg wash. Coat the bottom of the other long flap with egg wash. Press this flap down firmly to form a flat bottom for the samosa. Put the prepared samosa aside, folded-side down, while you repeat the process until all of the filling has been used.

Without crowding the pot or fryer, fry the samosas for 3 minutes, or until golden brown. Place on a paper towel–lined plate to drain.

Coriander Catfish Rolls

These rolls are served as an appetizer at Hong Kong House in Knoxville, Tennessee. They're one of the restaurant's best sellers, and they receive the most comments from both diners in Knoxville and those who learned to love them during chef Peter Chang's time in Atlanta.

The flavor of these rolls emphasizes coriander. The word cilantro *in the United States refers to the leaves of the coriander plant, but in Asia, the entire plant—seeds, roots, and leaves—is referred to as coriander. Coriander is a well-traveled herb that takes root wherever it lands. It's thought to have originated along the coast of the Mediterranean, based on references to it in the Bible and the discovery of seeds of the plant in Egyptian tombs. From there, it spread with the Romans to Europe and Asia, where it became a common addition to curries in India, Thailand, and Indonesia and was eaten as a green in China. It traveled with Europeans to the New World and took root in Latin American cuisine, where it adds flavor to salsas, soups, and sauces.*

There seems to be no middle ground when it comes to cilantro. Some people love the pungent tanginess it adds, but other people find that the flavor of the leaves reminds them of soap. Since like or dislike of the herb tends to run in families and cultures, it's likely that the flavor recognition of it is linked to genetics.

If you're among the fortunate people who like cilantro, these rolls are amazingly simple. Despite that simplicity, the combination of flavors and textures shows the true genius behind their creation. The tender fish provides an almost creamy backdrop for the tangy freshness of the cilantro leaves, and the moist filling is wrapped in crispy pastry. Altogether, the rolls provide a satisfying mixture of crunch, pungency, and richness that can't help but make you smile.

If you don't like coriander, don't rule out making these rolls with other herbs. Fresh parsley, thyme, or tarragon is a great substitute.

MAKES 4 DOZEN ROLLS

- 1 pound catfish fillets, minced
- 2 bunches cilantro, leaves and stems chopped
- 1 teaspoon lime juice
- 1 (1½-inch) piece ginger, grated
- 1 teaspoon coriander
- ½ teaspoon salt
- 48 (5-inch) spring roll wrappers

Heat at least 3 inches of soy or peanut oil to 375° in a deep pot or deep fryer.

In a large bowl, combine the catfish, cilantro, lime juice, ginger, coriander, and salt. Spread 1 teaspoon of the catfish mixture diagonally on a spring roll wrapper. Fold the wrapper over the catfish mixture to form a triangle. Using your index finger, tightly press the filling into a cylinder and roll the edges of the wrapper up to the filling. Leave the ends open. Repeat until all of the catfish mixture has been used.

Working in batches, carefully lower the rolls into the hot oil. Cook for 1–2 minutes, or until golden brown.

Catfish Fritters

Just as hushpuppies are favored in the South, fritters are popular worldwide. Fritters are fried batter mixed with fillings that range from apples in the United States to bananas in Myanmar. Savory ingredients get their due as well. Mushy pea fritters are popular in the United Kingdom. For us, it seemed only natural to incorporate an entire fried catfish meal into a fritter. The fritter itself is a hushpuppy, only this time instead of resting alongside catfish and fried okra, it's everything in one bite. Serve these with tartar sauce, and your guests will be begging for more.

MAKES 6–8 SERVINGS

- 1 pound catfish fillets, diced
- ½ cup stone-ground cornmeal
- ½ cup all-purpose flour
- 1 large yellow onion, minced
- 1 cup okra, sliced crosswise into thin disks
- 2 eggs
- 3 tablespoons buttermilk
- 1 teaspoon baking powder
- 2 teaspoons salt
- ¼ teaspoon freshly ground black pepper

Combine all ingredients in a large bowl to form a thick batter.

Heat at least 3 inches of soy or peanut oil to 350° in a deep pot or deep fryer.

Working in batches, drop the fritters by spoonfuls into the hot oil. Cook for 2–3 minutes, turning to ensure that all sides are golden brown. Place the fritters on a paper towel–lined plate to drain.

Mississippi Bao

When the Southern Foodways Alliance celebrated the global South at its 2010 symposium, chef Eddie Huang from Baohaus in New York was a guest chef. He presented pork belly bao as a Sunday brunch dish, one of his most famous creations, and rightly so.

Eddie's pork belly bao is his version of the traditional Taiwanese gua bao. It's street food—something that fits in your hand that you'll find everywhere in Taiwan. The dish is deceptively simple, though. The layering of flavors and textures is what makes it so delicious and what made us want to create our own version using catfish.

You'll notice that the first ingredient in the marinade is root beer. Yes, it's unorthodox, but it works. It adds a beautiful herbaceous quality to the sauce that complements the sweetness of the fish without overpowering it. Note, however, that not all root beers are created equal. You don't want to skimp here. The more complex the flavors of the root beer, the more complex the flavors of your sauce.

You'll need to plan ahead to serve these at your next party. The fish should marinate for at least 4 hours, and you may need time for the dough to thaw. You may find Szechuan peppercorns at the supermarket, but you're sure to find them, along with hot red bean paste, at most Asian markets. In the frozen section of Asian markets, you'll find an amazing variety of steamed buns. What you're looking for are plain Taiwanese buns, just a simple circle of dough folded in half. If you can't find them, white bread dough will work. The ingredients are the same—it's all just a matter of the cooking technique.

MAKES 16 BAO

FOR THE MARINADE
1 (12-ounce) can or bottle of root beer
1½ cups dark brown sugar
⅔ cup rice vinegar
2 teaspoons hot red bean paste
1 teaspoon Szechuan peppercorns
1 (⅓-inch) piece ginger, grated
1 garlic clove, crushed
1 teaspoon salt
2 tablespoons vegetable oil
1 pound catfish fillets

FOR THE BUNS
16 frozen plain Taiwanese buns or 1 pound frozen bread dough

TO FINISH
2 large radishes, shredded
1 medium carrot, shredded
1 bunch mint, chopped
1 small bunch cilantro, chopped
1 cup roasted peanuts, crushed

To make the marinade, in a small saucepan, combine the root beer, dark brown sugar, vinegar, red bean paste, peppercorns, ginger, garlic, and salt. Bring the mixture to a boil over high heat. Reduce the heat to medium and simmer until the glaze has thickened, about 20 minutes. Pour the glaze through a mesh strainer into a bowl, discarding any solids and reserving the liquid. Divide the liquid in half. Refrigerate half of the liquid to use as a sauce when serving. Whisk the oil into the remaining liquid to make the marinade.

Place the catfish fillets in a single layer in a baking dish. Pour the marinade over the catfish and cover the dish tightly with plastic wrap. Refrigerate for at least 4 hours or up to overnight.

To prepare the buns, if you're using frozen buns, steam them—in batches if necessary—in a parchment paper–lined steaming basket for 10–15 minutes, or until they're soft and pliable. After all the buns are cooked, turn off the heat under the steamer. Return all the buns to the steamer until ready to serve.

If you're using frozen bread dough, allow it to thaw completely at room temperature. Break off a 1-ounce piece of dough and roll it into a ball. Flatten the ball between 2 sheets of parchment paper to form a round of dough 4–5 inches in diameter. Fold the round in half to form a bun. Repeat with the remaining dough. Place the buns on a parchment paper–lined baking sheet and allow them to rest for 15 minutes. Turn them over and allow them to rest for 15 minutes more. Steam them in batches in a parchment paper–lined steaming basket for 3 minutes.

To make the catfish, warm the reserved sauce in a small saucepan over medium-low heat, stirring occasionally. Transfer the marinated fish to a wire rack placed over a baking sheet. Brush the fish generously with the warm sauce.

Preheat the broiler.

Cook the fish under the broiler for 6 minutes, or until the fillets have darkened and the edges are beginning to blacken.

To make the bao, roughly chop the catfish. Open a warm steamed bun and stuff with the catfish. Spoon the sauce over the fish before topping it with a sprinkling of radishes, carrot, mint, cilantro, and peanuts.

Smoky Catfish Mousse

Fish mousses have long been popular. Smoked salmon and cream cheese are an ideal match on bagels. Blend the two into a creamy spread with a little dill and chopped onion, and they get even better.

Sauce ravigote is a classic French sauce. Because it's creamy and lightly acidic, it's a perfect accompaniment for fish and seafood. Adding this sauce to the mix puts the combination of smoky catfish and cream cheese over the top.

When blending the ingredients together, pulse the food processor so you can stop when you achieve the texture you want. Serve this mousse with bagels, toast, or crackers. You can also use the sauce on boiled or sautéed shrimp, simply prepared fish (we humbly suggest catfish), or crab cakes.

MAKES 8–12 SERVINGS

FOR THE SAUCE RAVIGOTE

- 1 cup vegetable oil
- ½ cup extra-virgin olive oil
- ¼ cup apple cider vinegar
- 2 tablespoons Creole mustard
- 2 teaspoons minced shallots
- 2 teaspoons minced yellow onions
- 1 teaspoon capers
- 2 tablespoons minced parsley
- 2 teaspoons minced thyme
- 2 teaspoons salt
- 1 teaspoon freshly ground black pepper

FOR THE MOUSSE
2 pounds catfish fillets
8 slices hickory-smoked bacon
¼ cup minced yellow onions
2 tablespoons cream cheese
½ teaspoon salt
¼ teaspoon freshly ground black pepper

To make the sauce ravigote, combine all ingredients in a quart jar. Screw on the lid tightly and shake well until the sauce is thoroughly combined and no longer separates immediately after you stop shaking the jar.

To make the mousse, place the catfish and bacon in a small saucepan and cover with water. Bring to a boil over medium heat. Reduce the heat to a simmer and cook the catfish for 5–10 minutes, or until the fish flakes easily. Allow the fish to cool in the water. Drain and discard the bacon. Flake the fish with a fork, discarding any bones, skin, or fatty bits.

In a food processor, combine the catfish, onions, cream cheese, salt, pepper, and sauce ravigote. Process until the mousse is smooth and fluffy.

Smoky Catfish Brandade Spread

Andy Ticer and Michael Hudman are talented young chefs. Their first restaurant, Andrew Michael Italian Kitchen, and Hog & Hominy, its more casual sister restaurant across the street in East Memphis, both became dining destinations almost immediately. The chefs specialize in classic Italian cooking using southern ingredients.

A brandade is a traditional Mediterranean dish made from salt cod and potatoes. Andy and Michael use their smoker to cold-smoke catfish to make a southern version. This recipe brings the dish into your home kitchen by using smoked bacon and smoked paprika to impart flavor instead of having to use a smoker.

Serve the brandade with toasted rounds of hearty artisanal bread.

MAKES 6–8 SERVINGS

1 pound catfish fillets
4 slices hickory-smoked bacon
3 tablespoons butter, divided
1 medium onion, diced
½ teaspoon fresh thyme leaves
Salt
1 cup chicken broth
1 pound red potatoes, cubed
½ cup whipping cream
1 teaspoon smoked paprika

Place the catfish and bacon in a small saucepan and cover with water. Bring to a boil over medium heat. Reduce the heat to a simmer and cook the catfish for 5–10 minutes, or until the fish flakes easily. Allow the fish to cool in the water. Drain and discard the bacon. Flake the fish with a fork, discarding any bones, skin, or fatty bits.

Heat 2 tablespoons of the butter in a large skillet over medium heat. Add the onion, thyme, and a pinch of salt and cook, stirring frequently, until the onion has lightly browned, about 8 minutes. Transfer the onion mixture to a bowl.

In the same skillet, add the broth and potatoes and set the heat to medium-high. Bring the mixture to a boil, reduce the heat to low, and cover. Simmer the potatoes until they mash easily when gently pressed, about 15 minutes. Drain the potatoes.

Preheat the oven to 400°.

Add the onion mixture to a food processor and purée. Add the catfish and pulse until just combined.

Combine the potatoes and cream in a medium bowl. Mash by hand until the potatoes are creamy but the mixture still has texture. Season with salt to taste. Fold the onion and catfish mixture into the mashed potatoes.

Spread the mixture in a shallow buttered 1-quart casserole with a spatula, forming gentle peaks and not packing firmly. Dot the top of the brandade with the remaining 1 tablespoon butter and sprinkle evenly with the smoked paprika. Bake until light golden brown, 15–20 minutes.

Tea-Smoked Catfish

Smoked catfish is a beautiful thing, but if you don't have access to a smoker or the time and skill to use one, it seems out of reach. In other recipes, we've compensated for the lack of a smoker by cooking the fish with smoke-cured bacon and adding smoked paprika. But even without a smoker, the ingenuity of centuries of cooks can make it possible to smoke fish at home.

This is an Asian technique that's used not only for fish but also for any fat-rich meat that will easily absorb the flavors of the spice-laden smoke. Duck, chicken thighs, and pork belly are common targets. We chose catfish steaks for this recipe because of their uniform thickness. Steaks are also a more common cut in many Asian countries. Marinating the fish in salt and sake allows the sweetness of the sake to penetrate deeply into the meat. The sweetness is preserved by the brief steaming that cooks the fish.

When you're ready to smoke the fish, be brave. It's not hard as long as you have the right tools and take the right precautions. You need a wok for this, not just a deep pan or a Dutch oven. The shape of the wok makes the smoke circulate around the fish. The wok shouldn't be nonstick. You'll line the wok with aluminum foil before you start, but you're going to have to get the heat high to start the smoking process and Teflon can emit vapors at high heat. Look for a carbon steel or cast-iron wok instead. They're inexpensive and useful additions to your kitchen.

Once you have your wok, find a rack that will fit inside it to keep the fish above the smoldering tea. If you can't find a rack, chopsticks or bamboo skewers make a perfect rack in a pinch.

The most important thing aside from the wok itself is the lid. It doesn't have to seal tightly on its own; you're not going to find one that will. All you need is a lid that you can seal with aluminum foil that won't touch the fish beneath it. You can purchase lids for woks, but you can also improvise, just as you did for the rack. An inverted large stainless steel bowl can work, or you might be able to use the lid from a bamboo steamer.

Now, precautions. You're not going to burn down your house smoking catfish in your wok. But you do want to turn on the exhaust fan and open the windows. You're smoking something indoors, so there's a high probability that you'll set off your smoke detectors. Know this, be prepared, prepare others, and have at it. Once you've smoked your first catfish steak, you'll want to smoke more.

What you end up with is a complex blend of flavors. Catfish steaks have a firm texture that holds up well to this cooking method. The fish will be moist and sweet, while absorbing the rich tannins of the tea and the smoky aromatics of the jasmine rice and peppercorns. We recommend serving this either at room temperature or colder to best bring out the tannins. Edamame or a simple seaweed salad would be a lovely accompaniment, and a cup of light jasmine tea or warm sake would be perfect to set the mood.

MAKES 4 SERVINGS

---

4 large catfish steaks (about 2 pounds)

FOR THE MARINADE

⅓ cup sake
1 teaspoon salt

FOR SMOKING

½ cup jasmine rice
⅓ cup black tea leaves
1 teaspoon Szechuan peppercorns
1 teaspoon black peppercorns
1 teaspoon sugar

SPECIAL EQUIPMENT

Wok with a rack and a lid

To make the marinade, place the fish in a shallow container, add the sake, and sprinkle on the salt. Cover and refrigerate for 8 hours or up to a day, turning over at least once.

To steam the catfish, bring a large pot of water to a gentle boil over medium-high heat. Insert a steamer insert and lay the marinated fish gently on it. Steam the fish for 5–8 minutes, or until it begins to flake. Remove the fish from the steamer and allow it to cool to room temperature.

To smoke the catfish, line a wok with foil, being sure that it fits the wok tightly and has at least 2 inches of overhang all the way around. Add the rice, tea, peppercorns, and sugar to the wok, stirring to distribute evenly. Place a rack in the middle of the wok high enough to avoid touching the tea mixture in the bottom. Blot any moisture from the surface of the fish and place it on the rack. Cover the wok with a lid that doesn't touch the fish and seal it with the overhanging foil.

Turn an exhaust fan on high or open the windows. Set the wok on a burner over high heat for 5 minutes, or until you start to see wisps of smoke. Continue cooking for 5 more minutes. Turn the heat off sooner if you smell burning. Leaving the wok on the burner, turn off the heat and allow the wok to rest, sealed, for 7 minutes.

Soups and Stews

Catfish is versatile enough to appear in many dishes. Fried or broiled fillets make excellent sandwiches, but the tender meat also flakes finely enough to make creamy catfish salad. Catfish can substitute for almost any firm, white-fleshed fish, so it's a natural in soups and stews. Just like any other fish, don't let it cook too long or it will become tough.

The recipes in this chapter range from traditional to exotic, just to give you some idea of the flexibility catfish can offer. And if you're thinking that a fish soup sounds, well, fishy, just give some of these recipes a try. You'll be surprised at the way ginger brings out sweetness in the fish and at how well the texture of catfish contrasts with potatoes. It becomes a base of flavor for the heat of peppers and the tang of tomatoes without being lost in the mix.

Catfish Chowder

When most folks hear the word chowder, *their first thought is of rich, creamy New England clam chowder. But the main ingredient doesn't have to be limited to clams, and chowder is far older than New England. One theory is that the name of the dish evolved from the Latin word* calderia, *the root of the word* cauldron. *Another possible source of the name is the English word* jowter, *meaning fish peddler.*

Fish chowder recipes are found in the earliest American cookbooks, including The Virginia Housewife, *which has a chowder recipe that calls for "any kind of firm fish." Since catfish is our favorite firm fish and New England–style chowder is so good, we decided to combine them in this recipe.*

MAKES 6 SERVINGS

- 4 slices bacon, chopped
- 2 tablespoons butter, divided
- 1 tablespoon all-purpose flour
- 1 small white onion, diced
- 1 stalk celery, thinly sliced
- Salt
- 1 pound catfish fillets, cut into bite-sized pieces
- 3 medium red potatoes, peeled and diced
- ½ teaspoon fresh thyme leaves
- 1 bay leaf
- Freshly ground black pepper
- 1 cup dry white wine
- 2 cups whole milk
- 1 tablespoon chopped flat-leaf parsley

Cook the bacon in a large saucepan over medium heat. Place the bacon on a paper towel–lined plate to drain. Leave the drippings in the saucepan. Add 1 tablespoon of the butter to the drippings and melt. Add the flour and stir until combined. Add the onion, celery, and a pinch of salt. Cook, stirring constantly, for 5 minutes, or until the onion is translucent. Add the catfish, potatoes, thyme, bay leaf, 1 teaspoon salt, and ¼ teaspoon pepper. Add the wine and additional water if necessary to cover the fish and potatoes. Bring the liquid to a boil. Cover the saucepan, reduce the heat to low, and simmer for 15–20 minutes, or until the potatoes are soft. Add the milk and remaining 1 tablespoon butter. Crush half of the potatoes against the side of the pot to thicken the chowder.

Discard the bay leaf before serving. Add salt and pepper to taste. Sprinkle with parsley and crumbled bacon to serve.

Catfish Gumbo

Gumbo is the signature Cajun dish. The name has two possible sources. One is ki ngombo, *the Bantu word for okra, the podlike vegetable introduced by enslaved Africans. The other is* kombo, *the Choctaw word for filé, a powder made from grinding dried sassafras leaves. Okra and filé are both used to thicken different varieties of gumbo. A French roux, flour cooked in an equal amount of fat, is used to thicken gumbo as well.*

Each thickener adds its own unique flavor. This recipe goes all out, using a roux for thickness and the nutty flavor of browned flour as well as okra and filé for their flavors. Combining African, European, and Native American elements is what makes gumbo the most American of dishes—the ultimate melting pot.

MAKES 6 SERVINGS

---

1 pound andouille sausage, cut into 1-inch pieces
4 tablespoons lard, butter, or vegetable oil
4 tablespoons all-purpose flour
2 stalks celery, thinly sliced
1 medium yellow onion, chopped
1 small green bell pepper, chopped
Salt
2 garlic cloves, minced
2 cups water
1 (14.5-ounce) can whole peeled tomatoes
1½ cups sliced fresh or frozen okra
½ teaspoon Louisiana-style hot sauce
Freshly ground black pepper
Cayenne pepper
1 pound catfish fillets, cut into 1-inch pieces

TO SERVE
Cooked white rice
Filé powder

Cook the andouille in a large deep pot or Dutch oven over medium heat until brown and crisp. Remove the sausage and reserve, leaving any drippings in the pot. Add the lard, butter, or vegetable oil and allow it to melt. Add the flour and stir to combine until the mixture is smooth. Cook, stirring slowly and constantly, for 20–25 minutes, or until the roux is a milk chocolate color.

Add the celery, onion, bell pepper, and a pinch of salt to the roux and cook, stirring constantly, for another 5–7 minutes, or until the vegetables are soft. Add the garlic and continue cooking for another 2 minutes, or until the garlic is fragrant. Gradually add the water, stirring constantly to prevent lumps.

Increase the temperature to medium-high and bring the mixture to a boil. Add the tomatoes and okra, cover, and reduce the temperature to low. Simmer for 20 minutes, stirring occasionally to gently break up the tomatoes.

Add the hot sauce and season with salt, black pepper, and cayenne pepper to taste. Add the catfish and reserved andouille and continue to cook uncovered for 10 minutes.

Serve the gumbo with white rice and filé powder for each diner to add as desired.

Catfish-Rice Soup with Ginger and Onion
Cháo Cá

Cháo, *rice porridge, is one of the most popular dishes in Vietnam because it's a highly satisfying comfort food.* Cháo cá *is rice porridge with fish added. The type of fish used varies. We, of course, use catfish. We also add mung beans, a traditional Asian bean, for their healing properties since this soup is the Vietnamese equivalent of American chicken soup. You can find mung beans in health food stores, some supermarkets, and Asian markets and fish sauce in some supermarkets and Asian markets. This is the soup you want when you have a cold or a stomachache. Once you've tasted it, you'll understand why.*

MAKES 6 SERVINGS

- 1 (2-inch) piece ginger, thinly sliced
- 2 green onions, white parts only, chopped
- 3 tablespoons fish sauce, divided
- 1¼ teaspoons salt, divided
- 2 teaspoons sesame oil, divided
- ⅓ cup mung beans
- 1 pound catfish fillets, cut into 1-inch pieces
- 1 small red onion, minced
- 1 (2-inch) piece ginger, minced
- Juice of 1 lime
- ½ teaspoon sugar
- ⅓ cup short-grain white rice
- ½ cup chopped cilantro

In a medium deep pot, bring 6 cups of water to a boil over medium-high heat and add the sliced ginger, the green onions, 2 tablespoons of the fish sauce, and 1 teaspoon of the salt.

In a small skillet, heat 1 teaspoon of the sesame oil over medium heat and cook the mung beans, stirring constantly, until they're fragrant but not brown. Add the mung beans to the cooking liquid, reduce the heat to low, and simmer for 30 minutes.

While the beans are cooking, place the catfish in a shallow dish. In a small bowl, combine the remaining 1 tablespoon of fish sauce, the remaining ¼ teaspoon of salt, and the red onion, minced ginger, lime juice, and sugar, whisking gently to combine. Pour the mixture over the fish. Allow the fish to marinate at room temperature for 30 minutes.

Heat the remaining 1 teaspoon of sesame oil over low heat in the same skillet used to cook the mung beans. Stirring constantly, fry the rice until the grains are translucent and exude a nutty aroma but aren't brown. Add the rice to the soup and stir to combine. Cook the soup for another 25–30 minutes, stirring frequently to prevent sticking.

Add the fish to the soup and increase the heat to medium, stirring gently but constantly. When the soup comes to a boil, remove from the heat.

Garnish with cilantro before serving.

Nigerian Catfish Stew
Obe Eja

Fish is a popular ingredient in Nigeria. Because of its location on the Atlantic and the presence of the Niger River and its tributaries, both saltwater and freshwater fish abound, including catfish. The dish traditionally calls for catfish, obokun *in the Yoruba language, but other types of fish are sometimes used instead. We think catfish is ideal.*

Palm oil is an unusual ingredient, but you can find it in health food stores and larger supermarkets. It adds an earthy flavor and great depth to this simple stew, along with a beautiful orange color. Be careful when working with Scotch bonnet peppers, which are very hot. Be sure to wash your hands thoroughly after seeding them, especially before you place your hands anywhere near your face.

MAKES 6 SERVINGS

- 2 tablespoons peanut or canola oil
- 1 pound catfish fillets, cut into bite-sized pieces
- 1 small white onion, thinly sliced
- 2 large tomatoes, roughly chopped
- 2 Scotch bonnet peppers, seeded
- 1 large red bell pepper, quartered
- 1 large yellow onion, roughly chopped
- 1 (1-inch) piece ginger, roughly chopped
- 2 garlic cloves, chopped
- ½ cup water
- ½ cup palm oil
- 1 teaspoon fresh thyme leaves
- 1 teaspoon curry powder
- Salt
- 2 teaspoons chopped Thai basil

TO SERVE
Cooked white rice
Fried ripe plantains

Heat the peanut or canola oil in a large skillet over medium heat. Add the catfish and white onion and cook, turning often, until the fish is lightly browned on all sides and the onion is tender. Place the fish and onion on a paper towel–lined plate to drain.

In a blender or food processor, combine the tomatoes, Scotch bonnet peppers, bell pepper, yellow onion, ginger, garlic, and water. Blend or process until the mixture is completely liquefied.

Heat the palm oil in a large deep pot over high heat until it just begins to smoke. Carefully add the tomato mixture, which will splatter. Bring the mixture to a boil, cover, and reduce the heat to medium. Cook for 45 minutes, adding ½ cup water every 15 minutes if the mixture is getting dry.

Add the cooked fish and onion to the mixture along with the thyme, the curry powder, and 2 teaspoons salt, stirring gently to combine so the fish doesn't break apart. Cook, uncovered, for another 15 minutes. Season with salt to taste.

Sprinkle with basil right before serving. Serve with rice and fried plantains.

Indonesian Spicy-and-Sour Catfish Soup
Pindang Patin

A chain of over 17,000 islands in the Indian Ocean, Indonesia is the fourth most populous country in the world. The country is practically synonymous with coffee since it includes the islands of Java and Sumatra. This dish comes from Sumatra. Pindang *is the traditional spicy-and-sour soup of the region, and* patin *is Indonesian for silver catfish, one of the most popular river fish in Sumatra.*

Kecap manis, *sweet soy sauce, can be found in most Asian markets. If you can't find it, a reasonable substitution would be a half-and-half mixture of soy sauce and molasses. Tamarind paste can be found in Asian and Indian markets. There's really no substitute for the rich sweet-and-sour tang that tamarind gives the soup, so be sure to include it.*

MAKES 8 SERVINGS

- 6 shallots, roughly chopped
- 1 (2-inch) piece ginger, crushed
- 1 (2-inch) piece galangal, crushed
- 6 garlic cloves, chopped
- 3 stalks lemongrass, bulbs only, crushed
- 5 green tomatoes, cubed
- 3 ripe tomatoes, cubed
- 2 tablespoons light soy sauce
- 2 teaspoons lime juice
- 12 bird's-eye chili peppers, finely sliced
- $1/2$ ounce basil leaves, torn
- 3 tablespoons tamarind paste
- 2 tablespoons *kecap manis*

2 tablespoons light brown sugar
2 pounds catfish fillets, cut into bite-sized pieces
Salt, soy sauce, or fish sauce
Sugar

Using a mortar and pestle or food processor, crush or process the shallots, ginger, galangal, and garlic into a smooth paste. Bring 2 quarts of water to a boil in a large saucepan over medium heat. Add the garlic mixture and lemongrass and cook for 15 minutes. Add the tomatoes, soy sauce, and lime juice and continue boiling for 15 minutes. Add the chili peppers, basil, tamarind paste, *kecap manis*, and light brown sugar and continue boiling for 15 minutes. Add the catfish and continue cooking for 5 minutes, or until the fish is cooked through.

Remove the lemongrass stems before serving. Season with salt, soy sauce, or fish sauce and sugar to taste.

Szechuan Catfish Stew

Szechuan dishes have a reputation for heat, and this recipe is no exception. Hot bean sauce and dried hot peppers add considerable punch. The flavors of this dish are complex, in part because of a very interesting addition. Szechuan peppercorns add more than just a citrusy flavor; they create a chemical reaction on the tongue that numbs it (somewhat) to the pain of the heat.

Like most wok-cooked dishes, this stew comes together very quickly once you get started, so make sure you have all of your ingredients measured out and close at hand. Be especially mindful when cooking dried peppers in the wok. They can burn easily and not only taste bad but also give off fumes that will make your eyes water.

MAKES 4 SERVINGS

FOR THE MARINADE
1 egg white
2 tablespoons cornstarch
1 tablespoon Shaoxing wine (rice wine)
¼ teaspoon salt

FOR THE SOUP
1 pound catfish fillets, cut into roughly 2-inch pieces
2 cups shredded napa cabbage or bok choy
5 tablespoons peanut or vegetable oil, divided
2 tablespoons Szechuan hot bean sauce
6 garlic cloves, thinly sliced
6 green onions, chopped, divided
1 (1-inch) piece ginger, grated
1 cup Tien Tsin dried red peppers or other Szechuan peppers, divided
2 tablespoons Szechuan peppercorns
2 teaspoons light soy sauce

1 tablespoon Shaoxing wine
4 cups fish stock or water
1½ teaspoons salt

To make the marinade, in a large bowl, whisk together all ingredients. Add the fish, tossing to coat thoroughly. Allow the fish to rest in the marinade for 20–30 minutes while you prepare the remaining ingredients.

Arrange the napa cabbage in a 3–5-quart Dutch oven or clay pot set on the stove adjacent to your wok.

Heat 2 tablespoons of the peanut or vegetable oil in a wok over high heat. Carefully add the marinated fish in batches and cook for 2 minutes, or until the fish is just beginning to turn white. Place the fish on a paper towel–lined plate to drain, then spread it over the cabbage in the Dutch oven.

Heat another 2 tablespoons of the oil in the wok and add the hot bean sauce. Cook, stirring constantly, until fragrant, about 1 minute. Reduce the heat to medium and add the garlic, half of the green onions, the ginger, ½ cup of the dried peppers, and the Szechuan peppercorns and cook, continuing to stir, for 1–2 minutes, or until the garlic and ginger are fragrant. Be very careful not to let the peppercorns or peppers burn. Add the soy sauce and wine, stirring constantly, and cook for 1 more minute. Return the heat to high and add the fish stock or water and salt. Bring the soup to a boil and cook for 3 minutes.

Carefully pour the soup over the fish and cabbage in the Dutch oven. Immediately turn the burner beneath the Dutch oven to medium to keep the soup hot until serving.

Heat the remaining 1 tablespoon of oil in a medium skillet over medium heat. Add the remaining ½ cup dried peppers and cook for 1–2 minutes, or until the peppers are fragrant. Add the remaining green onions, stirring to combine. Pour the peppers and onions over the soup and serve.

Catfish Sauce Piquant

Sauce piquant is a traditional Cajun sauce. Normally it's served with shrimp or alligator, but catfish is certainly capable of taking on the starring role. This is a dish meant to be served when the whole family is getting together. It's cooked long and slow to allow the heat of the peppers to permeate the fish while everyone shares stories and the kids head outside to play.

This recipe reduces the cooking time and cuts back on the heat somewhat. It can cook longer as long as the catfish are added in the last 10–15 minutes. It can also be spicier. Just increase the amount of cayenne pepper. Add it a little at a time, though. A little goes a long way. The catfish marinates while you're preparing the other ingredients. If you want the fish to absorb more flavor from the marinade, it can rest overnight in the refrigerator.

MAKES 12–15 SERVINGS

FOR THE CATFISH
- 3 pounds catfish fillets, cut into bite-sized pieces
- 1 tablespoon white vinegar
- 2½ teaspoons salt
- 2 teaspoons freshly ground black pepper
- 2½ teaspoons cayenne pepper
- 1 tablespoon cold water

FOR THE SAUCE PIQUANT
- ¾ cup vegetable oil
- 1 cup all-purpose flour
- 2 large yellow onions, diced
- 2 stalks celery, diced
- 1 large green bell pepper, diced
- 4 garlic cloves, minced
- Salt
- 1 (10-ounce) can Ro-tel tomatoes

1 (8-ounce) can tomato sauce
1 (6-ounce) can tomato paste
1 teaspoon Worcestershire sauce
1 bay leaf
6 cups hot chicken stock or water
½ lemon
8 green onions, green parts only, chopped
¼ cup chopped flat-leaf parsley
Freshly ground black pepper

TO SERVE
Cooked white rice
Louisiana-style hot sauce

To make the catfish, in a large bowl, combine the catfish with the vinegar, salt, black pepper, cayenne pepper, and cold water, tossing to coat the fish evenly. Cover the bowl tightly and marinate at room temperature for 30 minutes to an hour while you prepare the vegetables. If desired, the catfish can be refrigerated overnight.

To make the sauce piquant, heat the oil in a large Dutch oven over medium-high heat. Add the flour and whisk constantly until the roux becomes slightly darker than peanut butter, 10–12 minutes. Add the onions, celery, bell pepper, garlic, and a pinch of salt. Reduce the heat to medium-low and cook, stirring frequently, for 5–8 minutes, or until the vegetables are tender and wilted. Add the Ro-tel tomatoes, tomato sauce, tomato paste, Worcestershire sauce, and bay leaf, stirring to combine. Cook for 5 more minutes. Add the hot chicken stock or water and lemon half.

Increase the heat to medium-high and bring the mixture to a rolling boil. Reduce the heat to a simmer and add ¼ of the marinated catfish. Cook, uncovered, for 30 minutes, stirring occasionally. Add more water if the sauce becomes too thick or the fish begins to stick to the bottom of the pot. Increase the heat to medium. Add the remaining catfish along with the green onions and parsley, stirring to combine well. Cook, uncovered, for an additional 10–15 minutes.

Remove the bay leaf and lemon half before serving. Season with salt and freshly ground black pepper to taste. Serve with white rice and hot sauce for each diner to add as desired.

Salads and Sandwiches

When most people think of a catfish sandwich, the New Orleans po'boy comes to mind. While the po'boy is a beautiful thing, there are many other possibilities for catfish. In this chapter, we feature all-American catfish sandwiches as well as some international favorites. We also provide catfish variations on a couple of classic salads.

Creamy Catfish-Pecan Salad

Chicken salad and tuna salad have long been southern staples. Chicken salad is a tasty way to use up leftover chicken, and tuna salad is easy because you can just pop open a can. Catfish also makes an easy and inexpensive salad. This recipe has it all—creaminess and crunch, sweetness and richness. After poaching and flaking the catfish, you can use the meat in your favorite salad recipe. You can tweak this recipe by adding fresh herbs, spices like smoked paprika, or spice blends like garam masala.

Pecan oil is a little hard to come by, but due to its growing popularity, you may be able to find it at your local pecan grower, health food store, or organic market. Just be aware that you'll need to refrigerate it or use it quickly after opening it because it will go rancid if left at room temperature for very long.

MAKES 6–8 SERVINGS

- 1 teaspoon black peppercorns
- 1 bay leaf
- 2 pounds catfish fillets
- ¼ cup pecan oil
- ½ cup pecan halves
- 1 cup mayonnaise
- 1 Granny Smith apple, diced
- 1 medium onion, diced
- ½ teaspoon mustard powder
- 1 teaspoon salt
- ½ teaspoon freshly ground black pepper

Preheat the oven to 350°.

To make the catfish, bring 4 cups of water, the peppercorns, and the bay leaf to a boil over high heat in a large saucepan. Add the catfish and pecan oil and reduce the heat to low. Cover the saucepan and simmer for 12–15 minutes, or until the fish is no longer translucent and begins to flake. Remove the fish from the poaching liquid. Using a fork, flake the fish into small pieces and allow it to cool for 15 minutes.

While the fish is cooling, line a baking sheet with parchment paper and spread the pecans on the baking sheet in a single layer. Toast the pecans in the oven for 10 minutes, tossing after 5 minutes. Remove the pecans from the oven and allow them to cool to room temperature.

In a large bowl, combine the mayonnaise, apple, onion, and catfish. Add the mustard powder, salt, and pepper, stirring to blend thoroughly. Roughly chop the pecans and stir them into the salad.

Serve on a sandwich with lettuce and tomato or with crackers as a dip.

Grilled Catfish Salad

The invention of salads topped with meat was brilliant. "It's not fried chicken. It's a salad*!" For this salad, the catfish is a healthy choice since it isn't deep-fried. This salad shows off the versatility of catfish by pairing it with the Mediterranean flavors of oranges, red onions, feta cheese, and olives.*

MAKES 4 SERVINGS

FOR THE DRESSING
- ⅔ cup extra-virgin olive oil
- ½ cup apple cider vinegar
- ⅓ cup orange juice
- 1 teaspoon lemon juice
- ½ teaspoon honey
- ½ teaspoon salt
- ¼ teaspoon freshly ground black pepper

FOR THE CATFISH
- 2 tablespoons extra-virgin olive oil
- Zest of 1 medium orange
- 2 teaspoons lemon juice
- ½ teaspoon salt
- ¼ teaspoon freshly ground black pepper
- 4 small catfish fillets (about 1 pound)

FOR THE SALAD
- 8 ounces baby spinach
- Segments of 2 medium oranges, supremed
- 1 medium red onion, chopped
- 4 ounces feta cheese, crumbled
- 1 cup pitted black olives, drained
- 1 cup toasted pine nuts

To make the dressing, in a small bowl, whisk together all ingredients until well combined. Taste for seasoning and adjust as necessary.

To make the catfish, in a small bowl, whisk together the olive oil, orange zest, lemon juice, salt, and pepper. Coat each side of the catfish fillets.

Heat a grill pan over medium-high heat. Carefully spread oil on the pan with a paper towel, then place the fillets on the pan. Allow them to cook, undisturbed, for 3–4 minutes, or until the fillets no longer stick to the pan. Flip the fillets and cook the other side for another 3–4 minutes. Place the fish on a plate and tent with foil to keep warm.

To assemble the salad, divide the spinach between 4 large salad bowls. Top each salad with a grilled fish fillet and scatter over the remaining ingredients. Drizzle generously with the dressing and serve.

Catfish Po'Boys

A po'boy is the New Orleans version of a submarine sandwich or hoagie. The primary difference is the bread. New Orleans-style French bread is similar to a baguette, but it's larger in diameter and has a crispy exterior and a fluffy interior. If you're unable to find New Orleans-style French bread, a hoagie roll will do.

The name po'boy *is thought to stem from a 1929 New Orleans streetcar strike. During the strike, former streetcar conductors Benny and Clovis Martin served the strikers sandwiches from their restaurant for free. The restaurant staff is said to have called the strikers "poor boys," and the term became associated with the sandwich.*

MAKES 4 SERVINGS

FOR THE CATFISH

1 egg
1 cup buttermilk
1 teaspoon Louisiana-style hot sauce
1 cup cornmeal
1 teaspoon Cajun seasoning
1 teaspoon salt
$1/2$ teaspoon freshly ground black pepper
$1/4$ teaspoon cayenne pepper (optional)
4 catfish fillets (about 1 pound)

FOR THE PO'BOYS

2 loaves New Orleans-style French bread
Mayonnaise
Creole mustard
$1/2$ head lettuce, shredded
Sliced dill pickles
1 large tomato, halved and sliced

To make the catfish, heat at least 3 inches of soy or peanut oil to 375° in a deep pot or deep fryer.

In a medium bowl, whisk together the egg, buttermilk, and hot sauce.

In a shallow bowl, stir together the cornmeal, Cajun seasoning, salt, black pepper, and cayenne pepper, if using, to evenly distribute the seasonings.

Dip a fillet into the buttermilk mixture, being sure that both sides are coated. Allow any excess to drip back into the bowl. Dredge the fillet through the seasoned cornmeal, coating it evenly on both sides.

Gently lower the prepared fillet into the hot oil. Allow it to cook for 5–7 minutes, or until the coating is golden brown on both sides and the flesh is firm. Carefully flip the fillet if necessary. Place the fillet on a paper towel–lined plate to drain and repeat the process with the remaining fillets. Be sure to allow the oil to return to 375° before adding a new piece of fish. Tent the cooked fish with aluminum foil to keep warm.

To make the po'boys, halve the baguettes and split them open. Lightly toast them until the crusts are crisp and the insides are warm. Lightly spread mayonnaise and mustard on each slice of bread. Make a bed of shredded lettuce on each of the bottom slices and top with dill pickle slices. Top each with a cooked catfish fillet and then tomato slices. Cover with the top slice of bread. Cut each po'boy in half on a diagonal and serve.

Catfish Burgers

With its moist, flaky texture, catfish makes a great substitute for crab in crab cake recipes. Instead of getting fancy, this recipe makes hearty patties perfect for burgers. You could plate these as catfish cakes—a dollop of tartar sauce and you're set—but that just wouldn't be as much fun.

The flavors here are simple and may be familiar to some of you. These burgers are based on the famous shrimp burgers of the South Carolina coast.

MAKES 4 SERVINGS

1 pound catfish fillets, diced
2 eggs, beaten
1 cup panko breadcrumbs
3 tablespoons mayonnaise
2 tablespoons diced celery
1 tablespoon grated sweet onions
2 tablespoons chopped parsley
$1\frac{1}{2}$ teaspoons lemon zest
1 teaspoon Worcestershire sauce
Salt and freshly ground black pepper
Cayenne pepper
3 tablespoons peanut or vegetable oil

TO SERVE
4 large hamburger buns
Lettuce
Tomato slices
Tartar sauce (page 27) or coleslaw (page 28)

In a medium bowl, combine the catfish, eggs, panko, mayonnaise, celery, onions, parsley, lemon zest, and Worcestershire sauce, stirring with a wooden spoon until everything is evenly distributed. Season with salt, black pepper, and cayenne pepper to taste. Divide the mixture into 4 equal portions and form patties about 1 inch thick.

Heat the oil in a large skillet over medium heat. Cook the patties for 4 minutes, or until the bottoms are browned, before carefully flipping them over. Cook for another 4 minutes so both sides are browned.

Serve on soft buns with lettuce, tomato, and tartar sauce or coleslaw.

Catfish Tacos

Fish tacos are a delicious treat from southern California and the Baja Peninsula of Mexico. This recipe takes a more southern approach. Traditional fish tacos have larger chunks of cabbage, while these tacos have a finer shredded slaw. Fish tacos also use breaded cubes of cod or other white fish. Here the unbreaded catfish makes a difference not only in flavor but also in appearance. The catfish pieces curl up in the skillet to resemble shrimp, while the chili powders tint them dark red. Check local Hispanic markets or tortillerias for the freshest corn tortillas you can get. Nestled in a good tortilla, the combination of cool slaw and hot fish is irresistible.

MAKES 4 SERVINGS

FOR THE SLAW
- 1 jalapeño, seeded and diced
- 1 bunch cilantro, chopped
- 1¼ cups mayonnaise
- Juice of 1 lime
- ½ head cabbage, shredded
- Salt

FOR THE TACOS
- 1 tablespoon vegetable oil
- 1 pound catfish, cut into bite-sized pieces
- 1 teaspoon chili powder
- ¼ teaspoon ancho chili powder
- ¼ teaspoon garlic powder
- ¼ teaspoon salt

TO SERVE

8 hot corn tortillas
Sliced avocados
Diced onions
Mexican hot sauce
1 lime, quartered

To make the slaw, in a food processor, combine the jalapeño and cilantro. Process until finely puréed. Add the mayonnaise and lime juice and continue processing until just combined.

Place the cabbage in a large bowl and pour the mayonnaise mixture over it, stirring to coat the cabbage thoroughly. Add salt to taste.

To make the tacos, heat the oil in a large skillet over medium heat. Add the catfish to the skillet and sprinkle with the chili powder, ancho chili powder, garlic powder, and salt. Cook for 5 minutes, stirring constantly.

To serve, place ⅛ of the catfish on a heated corn tortilla. Top with a generous spoonful of the slaw, avocados, onions, and hot sauce. Serve each diner 2 tacos garnished with a lime quarter.

TIP ❋ If you have a gas stove, you can heat the corn tortillas over an open flame for a more authentic taqueria flavor. Lay a tortilla flat on a burner set on medium heat. Flip the tortilla with tongs after 15 seconds and let the other side warm for another 15 seconds. You'll end up with soft, warm tortillas with lightly charred crisp spots.

Catfish *Bánh Mì*

In New Orleans, bánh mì *are known as Vietnamese po'boys. In Vietnam,* bánh mì *refers to the bread that was introduced to the country by the French. In areas where Vietnamese refugees have settled, the term has come to mean a sandwich made on that bread. The comparison to a po'boy is apt. Besides the bread, the two sandwiches have other similarities, including an emphasis on pickles and having meat as a main ingredient.*

One interesting example of the Vietnamese influence on New Orleans is Dong Phuong Bakery. Since it opened in 1981, the bakery has become one of the city's largest suppliers of bread, especially to restaurants serving bánh mì*. The Dong Phuong Restaurant doesn't serve catfish* bánh mì*, but that variation can be found elsewhere in the area.*

In the marinade for the catfish, you can use honey or cane syrup, which will caramelize when the fish is cooked under the broiler. While honey is easier to come by, it's worth keeping an eye out for Steen's cane syrup from Louisiana because it will add a little something extra to these great sandwiches.

You'll be making your own pickled vegetables for this recipe. While they only require 30 minutes of resting time before serving, the longer you store them, the better the flavors will be.

MAKES 4 SERVINGS

FOR THE PICKLED VEGETABLES
- 1 cup rice vinegar
- ½ cup water
- 2 tablespoons sugar
- 1 tablespoon salt
- 1 (8-ounce) daikon radish, cut into 1-inch matchsticks
- 1 (8-ounce) cucumber, peeled, seeded, and cut into 1-inch matchsticks
- 1 medium carrot, cut into 1-inch matchsticks

FOR THE CATFISH
2 green onions, minced
1 (2-inch) piece ginger, minced
2 tablespoons light soy sauce
2 teaspoons fish sauce
1 tablespoon toasted sesame oil
1 tablespoon honey or cane syrup
1 garlic clove, minced
1 pound catfish fillets

FOR THE DRESSING
¼ cup mayonnaise
1 tablespoon sriracha
1 teaspoon lemon juice

FOR THE BÁNH MÌ
1 baguette, cut into 4 pieces
1 bunch cilantro
1 jalapeño or serrano pepper, thinly sliced (optional)

To make the pickled vegetables, combine the vinegar, water, sugar, and salt in a medium bowl, stirring until the sugar and salt are dissolved. Add the radish, cucumber, and carrot and stir to coat thoroughly. Cover the bowl tightly and refrigerate for at least 30 minutes before using.

To make the catfish, place the green onions, ginger, soy sauce, fish sauce, sesame oil, honey or cane syrup, and garlic in a shallow dish, stirring to combine. Add the catfish fillets and turn to coat completely. Cover the dish tightly and refrigerate for at least 20 minutes.

Heat the broiler to high.

Lightly grease a baking sheet and arrange the marinated catfish fillets on it in a single layer. Cook them under the broiler for 6 minutes, or until the fish flakes easily with a fork.

To make the dressing, place all ingredients in a small bowl, stirring to combine. Taste to judge the heat level, adding more sriracha if you like.

To make the *bánh mì*, slice open the baguette pieces and toast the inside lightly for 1 minute under the broiler. Spread the dressing on each slice of bread. Fill each sandwich with fish, drained pickled vegetables, a generous handful of cilantro, and slices of jalapeño or serrano pepper, if desired.

Entrées

Catfish is the center of meals around the world, providing us with bountiful preparation methods. In this chapter, we look at traditional catfish dishes from the United States, the Caribbean, South America, Europe, Africa, and Asia. In addition, we've taken inspiration from these traditional dishes to create new dishes, which are a melding of exotic approaches with good old southern sensibilities.

Baked Catfish with Citrus

Fish and citrus are a natural combination. A good squeeze of lemon juice brightens the flavor of fish. Even the most hole-in-the-wall, out-of-the-way places wouldn't dare send out a plate of catfish without a wedge of lemon. This dish comes to the table with the citrus flavor already incorporated, along with an herbal undertone. Serve this on a bed of wild rice or rice pilaf to catch the buttery sauce.

MAKES 4 SERVINGS

FOR THE CATFISH

1½ tablespoons extra-virgin olive oil, divided
4 small whole catfish (about 2 pounds)
1 teaspoon freshly ground black pepper
1 teaspoon coarse sea salt
1 teaspoon minced shallots
1 tablespoon each roughly chopped rosemary, sage, and chives
8 slices lemon
8 slices lime
8 slices tangerine

FOR THE BUTTER SAUCE

2 tablespoons extra-virgin olive oil
2 tablespoons flour
1 teaspoon kosher salt
1 teaspoon lemon juice
1 cup water
1 tablespoon butter

Preheat the oven to 400°.

To make the catfish, lightly coat a 9 × 13-inch baking dish with ½ tablespoon of the olive oil and place the fish in it with the cavities facing each other. Pour 1 tablespoon of the olive oil over the fish and rub it on both sides of each fish. Sprinkle the inside and outside of each fish with the pepper, sea salt, and shallots. Stuff the herbs into the cavity of each fish along with 1 slice of each type of citrus fruit. Arrange the remaining slices of fruit on top of each fish.

To make the butter sauce, heat the olive oil in a small saucepan over medium heat. Add the flour and kosher salt and stir to combine. Cook, stirring constantly, for 2 minutes, or until the flour is cooked but not brown. Increase the heat to medium-high. Add the lemon juice and water and continue stirring for another 5–7 minutes, or until the sauce is thick and bubbly. Stir in the butter and remove the sauce from the heat. Pour the sauce around but not over the fish in the baking dish. Bake the fish, uncovered, for 20–25 minutes, or until the fish flakes easily with a fork.

Butter-Poached-Catfish Surf and Turf

Surf and turf is an undeniable symbol of decadence. But even it can be improved by adding a southern twist. Here, rather than roaring surf, we have the waters of southern rivers—and many a farm pond—lapping at the bank. And while we do have cattle grazing on turf, we also have something equally good: deer foraging in the wild.

Venison is a wonderful meat that many people have never had the opportunity to enjoy. It's much leaner than beef, but it has a similar flavor, though it's slightly stronger. If you're not a hunter, you can still get venison by ordering it through a specialty grocer. Also, many local butchers now process deer from local hunters. If you prefer, though, you can substitute beef or pork tenderloin for the venison. Although catfish isn't as sweet as lobster, poaching it in butter makes it so good you won't care that it's not lobster.

MAKES 2 SERVINGS

FOR THE VENISON
2 tablespoons extra-virgin olive oil
⅓ cup black peppercorns
2 venison tenderloins (about ½ pound each)
Salt
1 shallot, minced
¼ cup red wine
¼ cup chicken stock
1 tablespoon butter

FOR THE CATFISH
2 small catfish fillets (about ½ pound)
1 stick butter
5 tablespoons water
½ teaspoon salt

1 tablespoon fresh thyme leaves
1 teaspoon lemon juice
Freshly ground black pepper

To make the venison, heat the olive oil in a large skillet over medium heat. While the oil is heating, roughly crush the peppercorns in a mortar and pestle or spice grinder. Sprinkle the tenderloins with salt and then roll them in the crushed peppercorns. Sear the tenderloins in the heated skillet for 2 minutes before turning. Repeat until all sides have browned and the center is medium-rare. Transfer the tenderloins to a platter and tent with foil to keep warm and allow them to rest.

Add the shallot to the skillet and cook, stirring constantly, until translucent, about 3 minutes. Slowly add the wine and chicken stock to the skillet. Stir to loosen any bits from the bottom of the skillet. Raise the heat to high. Stirring constantly, cook until the sauce thickens and reduces by half. Add the butter and whisk until melted. Season with salt to taste. Remove the sauce from the heat. Cover to keep warm.

To make the catfish, cut each fillet lengthwise into 2 pieces. Cut the butter into 16 equal slices.

Bring the water to a boil over high heat in a small saucepan. Add 4 slices of the butter, whisking to combine. Reduce the heat to low and add the remaining butter slices, whisking constantly, until a thick sauce forms. Add the salt and stir until dissolved.

Place the catfish in a single layer in an empty saucepan off the heat. Pour the butter mixture over the fish. Place the catfish over low heat and cook it until it's opaque, 12–15 minutes, flipping once during cooking. Carefully remove the fish from the butter mixture and set aside. Add the thyme, lemon juice, and pepper to the butter mixture, whisking to combine.

To assemble each dish, slice a venison tenderloin into 8 medallions and arrange on one side of the plate. Drizzle with the pan sauce. Gently place 2 catfish tenderloins on the other side of the plate. Drizzle generously with the butter and herb sauce.

Maple Planked Catfish

Grilling fish on a plank of fragrant wood seems like a high-end-restaurant type of thing to do. And there are plenty of classy restaurants that use the technique. But it originated with the native people of the northwest United States who saw the advantage of using the wood to protect the delicate flesh of fish from the open flame while imparting its aromatic qualities to the fish.

It's a perfect technique for catfish, and if it's too cold to grill, this recipe works just as well in the oven. Plan ahead, though. Whether you're cooking on a grill or in the oven, you need to soak the planks before you cook on them. If you cook on dry planks, you risk catching them on fire, and even if they don't burn the fish, the acrid smoke they produce will ruin the flavor.

The sauce is a play on the sweet barbecue sauces of the South without the addition of tomato, which would be too heavy for the fish. The maple syrup creates an amber glaze that holds the seasonings and caramelizes beautifully on the fish. We recommend serving this with garlicky mashed potatoes and creamed spinach for a well-rounded meal. You can even serve the meal on the planks for a unique presentation.

MAKES 4 SERVINGS

FOR THE SAUCE

- 1 cup maple syrup
- 2 tablespoons butter
- 1 (1½-inch) piece ginger, grated
- 1 tablespoon soy sauce
- 1 tablespoon lemon juice
- 1 teaspoon paprika
- ¼ teaspoon freshly ground black pepper
- ¼ teaspoon cayenne pepper
- 1 tablespoon cornstarch
- 2 tablespoons water

FOR THE CATFISH
Vegetable oil
4 catfish fillets (about 1 pound)

SPECIAL EQUIPMENT
4 cedar grilling planks

Prepare the grilling planks by soaking them in warm water for 2 hours. Weigh them down with a heavy pot to keep them fully submerged.

To make the sauce, combine the maple syrup and butter in a medium saucepan over medium heat, stirring frequently until the butter is melted. Add the ginger, soy sauce, lemon juice, paprika, black pepper, and cayenne pepper, stirring to combine.

Dissolve the cornstarch in the water. Bring the sauce to a boil and stir in the cornstarch mixture. Simmer, stirring frequently, until the sauce has thickened.

To make the catfish, brush one side of each plank lightly with vegetable oil. Pat the catfish dry with a paper towel. Place each fillet on the oiled side of each plank and brush with the sauce to coat. Place the cedar planks over indirect heat on the grill or in a 350° oven. If grilling, close the lid of the grill and cook for 30 minutes, or until the fish flakes easily. If cooking in the oven, bake for 20 minutes. Brush lightly with more sauce to serve.

Blackened Catfish

New Orleans chef Paul Prudhomme popularized the method of blackening fish. Cooking the dish properly does mean blackening the fish. An extremely hot pan and a deft touch create a crispy piece of fish with seared-in spices. The method in this recipe is a slight variation on the way the dish is made in restaurants that will help prevent burning the fish. The texture and flavor remain unchanged. Serve with a New Orleans favorite like dirty rice or maque choux.

MAKES 4 SERVINGS

- 1 tablespoon onion powder
- 2 teaspoons thyme
- 1 teaspoon paprika
- 1 teaspoon oregano
- 1/2 teaspoon sugar
- 1/2 teaspoon salt
- 1/2 teaspoon freshly ground black pepper
- 1/2 teaspoon white pepper
- 1/4 teaspoon cayenne pepper
- 4 large catfish fillets (about 2 pounds)
- 2 tablespoons extra-virgin olive oil
- 1 garlic clove, crushed
- 1 tablespoon butter
- 1 lemon, halved

In a small bowl, combine the onion powder, thyme, paprika, oregano, sugar, salt, black pepper, white pepper, and cayenne pepper. Whisk to distribute evenly. Sprinkle the spice mixture evenly over both sides of the fillets, coating them well.

Heat the olive oil in a large skillet over medium-high heat. Cook the garlic, stirring constantly, until golden brown and very fragrant. Remove the garlic and discard. Add the butter and allow it to melt and foam. Add the seasoned catfish fillets and cook for 4 minutes. Gently flip the fillets and cook the other side for 4 minutes.

Transfer the cooked fillets to a serving dish and squeeze the lemon halves over them.

Jerk Catfish

In 1655, Britain invaded Jamaica, and the Spanish colonists fled, leaving their slaves behind. The slaves took the opportunity to escape into the surrounding mountains, where they met the local Taíno tribe. Jerk seasoning resulted from a combination of the culinary traditions of the former slaves and the available ingredients on the island. The word jerk *is thought to have evolved from the word* charqui, *the Spanish spelling of a Quechuan word for jerked or dried meat. The same word became* jerky *in English.*

Jerk seasoning can be found in most grocery stores now, but nothing is better than creating the exact blend of spices to suit your own tastes.

The relish in this recipe provides a sweet counter to the heat of the jerk.

MAKES 4 SERVINGS

FOR THE RELISH
- 1 pineapple, diced
- 2 medium ripe mangoes, diced
- 1 Thai chili pepper, seeded and sliced into thin rings
- 1 bunch green onions, chopped
- 1 bunch cilantro, chopped
- Juice of 1 lime
- 1 teaspoon light brown sugar
- ½ teaspoon yellow curry powder
- ½ teaspoon salt

FOR THE CATFISH
- 2½ teaspoons vegetable oil
- ½ teaspoon white vinegar
- 1 small yellow onion, chopped
- 1 jalapeño, seeded and chopped
- 1 (1-inch) piece ginger, minced
- 1 garlic clove, chopped

2 teaspoons dark brown sugar
1½ teaspoons allspice
1½ teaspoons thyme
½ teaspoon grated nutmeg
1 teaspoon salt
¼ teaspoon freshly ground black pepper
¼ teaspoon cayenne pepper
6 catfish fillets (about 1½ pounds), halved lengthwise

TO SERVE
Cooked white rice

To make the relish, combine all ingredients in a medium bowl and toss to combine. Cover and refrigerate for at least 30 minutes to allow the flavors to combine and develop.

To make the catfish, preheat the broiler.

In a blender or food processor, combine all ingredients except the catfish and pulse until a smooth paste forms.

Line a baking sheet with aluminum foil and arrange the catfish pieces on it. Smear the paste generously over the top of each piece. Cook the catfish under the broiler for 6 minutes, or until the spice mixture forms a crisp crust and the fish is opaque and flaky.

Serve with white rice. Place the relish in a serving bowl for diners to add as they like.

Colombian Catfish Pie
Pastel de Bagre y Papa

Colombia is a beautiful country with a range of landscapes. From the interior, the Andes Mountains sweep down through rainforest before reaching the Caribbean Sea to the north and the Pacific Ocean to the south. Potatoes are native to the Andes, and catfish swim in the country's rivers. This recipe makes the most of Colombia's rich bounty.

This dish is more like a casserole than a pie. The potatoes and catfish are layered with a rich cream sauce and topped with breadcrumbs and parmesan cheese, which bake into a crisp crust. Serve slices with a fresh green salad.

MAKES 8 SERVINGS

- 6 medium waxy potatoes, peeled and thinly sliced
- 4 tablespoons butter
- 1 medium yellow onion, thinly sliced
- 2 garlic cloves, minced
- 1 cup heavy whipping cream
- Salt and freshly ground black pepper
- 2 eggs, beaten
- 1 pound catfish fillets, cut into bite-sized pieces
- ½ tablespoon cumin
- ½ tablespoon paprika
- 1 cup breadcrumbs
- ½ cup grated parmesan cheese
- 2 green onions, thinly sliced

Preheat the oven to 400°. Grease a 9 × 13-inch baking dish.

Bring a large pot of lightly salted water to a boil. Add the potatoes and cook for 7 minutes, or until the potatoes are tender. Drain.

In a large skillet over medium-high heat, melt the butter. Add the onion and cook, stirring frequently, until translucent, about 5 minutes. Add the garlic and cook for 2 minutes, or until the garlic is fragrant. Add the cream and season with salt and pepper to taste. Bring the mixture to a boil, reduce the heat to low, and simmer for 5 minutes. Allow the mixture to cool, then add the beaten eggs.

Season the catfish with the cumin and paprika and salt and pepper to taste.

Assemble the pie by spreading half of the potatoes in the bottom of the prepared baking dish. Top with half of the onion and cream mixture. Place the catfish on top of the onions. Top with the remaining potatoes, then the rest of the onion and cream mixture. Sprinkle the top with breadcrumbs and parmesan cheese. Bake for 25–30 minutes, or until golden brown on top.

Garnish with the green onions to serve.

Catfish *en Papillote*

En papillote *is French for "in parchment." It's a classic cooking method in which food is placed in a folded parcel and then baked so the moisture in the parcel steams the food inside. It's a great technique to use with catfish, which takes on the flavors of the sauce and herbs beautifully as it steams.*

Let this be the star of the table. Serve the fish in the unopened parcels so each diner can experience the rush of heady aromatic steam upon opening the parcel. Keep the side dish simple — crispy sautéed haricots verts or courgettes are a perfect light accompaniment.

MAKES 4 SERVINGS

- 4 tablespoons butter
- 3 tablespoons dry sherry
- 1 tablespoon Worcestershire sauce
- 2 tablespoons chopped green onions
- 1 garlic clove, minced
- ½ teaspoon salt
- ½ teaspoon freshly ground black pepper
- 16 sprigs thyme
- 4 large catfish fillets (about 2 pounds)
- 2 ounces ham, julienned
- 8 lemon slices

Preheat the oven to 450°.

Combine the butter, sherry, and Worcestershire sauce in a small saucepan over medium-low heat. Cook, stirring frequently, until the butter is melted. Add the green onions, garlic, salt, and pepper, stirring to combine. Remove the sauce from the heat.

Cut 4 sheets of parchment paper 18 inches long. Fold each sheet in half lengthwise. Open up each piece of parchment paper and place 4 sprigs of thyme along the fold. Lay a catfish fillet over the thyme. Top the fillet with ¼ of the ham and 2 lemon slices. Bring the two sides of the parchment paper together and, leaving the top edges open, fold over the outside edges several times, sealing as tightly as possible. Gently spoon ¼ of the sauce into the opening at the top of each parcel, then fold the top over several times to seal tightly, leaving room above the fish for steam to rise. Place the parcels on a baking sheet. Bake for 10–12 minutes.

Serve the fish in the unopened parcels.

Delta Paella

Paella is a rice-based dish created in the Valencia region along the Mediterranean coast of Spain. In Spain, the dish either looks inland for rabbit and sausage or to the sea for seafood. In this version, you don't have to look too far beyond the Mississippi Delta to find most of the ingredients, and nearly everything you need is raised, grown, or caught in the South.

MAKES 8–10 SERVINGS

- 2 cups chicken broth
- 1 pinch saffron threads
- 1 pound catfish, cut into bite-sized pieces
- 12 large freshwater prawns or shrimp
- Salt
- 2 tablespoons minced parsley
- 8 garlic cloves, minced
- 1 tablespoon fresh thyme leaves
- 2 teaspoons smoked paprika
- 4 tablespoons pecan oil
- 1 red bell pepper, diced
- 1 medium yellow onion, diced
- 3 green onions, chopped
- 1 large tomato, cubed
- 1 cup short-grain rice, preferably arborio
- ½ cup green peas
- 1 dozen mussels
- 1 pint shucked oysters, drained
- Lemon wedges

Heat the broth in a large pot over low heat. Add the saffron and stir. Allow the broth to simmer while you prepare the remaining ingredients.

Pat the catfish and prawns dry between paper towels. Sprinkle them with salt and let them rest for 10 minutes.

In a mortar and pestle, mash together the parsley, garlic, and thyme and ⅛ teaspoon salt into a paste. Stir in the paprika. Add water by drops, if necessary, to form a paste.

Heat the oil in a large shallow skillet or paella pan over medium heat. Add the bell pepper, onion, and green onions and a pinch of salt and cook for 5 minutes, or until the vegetables are slightly softened. Increase the heat to medium-high and add the tomato and a pinch of salt. Cook for 5 minutes, or until the tomato breaks down and becomes saucelike in consistency. Carefully pour in the broth and bring the mixture to a boil.

Sprinkle the rice evenly into the pan and add 4 teaspoons salt. Boil for 3 minutes, stirring the rice and rotating the skillet occasionally. Stir in the parsley paste, then stop stirring after this point. Reduce the heat to medium-low and continue to simmer, uncovered, for 10 minutes, or until most of the liquid has been absorbed by the rice.

Arrange the catfish, prawns, peas, and mussels over the top, with the side of the mussel shells that will open after cooking pointing up. Increase the heat to medium and cook, uncovered, for 15–20 minutes, or until the rice is almost done. Reduce the heat to low. Scatter the oysters over the rice and cover the pan with foil. Let the paella cook for 10 minutes. Discard any mussels that didn't open.

Garnish with lemon wedges to serve.

Mediterranean-Style Steamed Catfish

This recipe combines some of the finest flavors of the Mediterranean. The vegetables begin to cook when you sauté them, and they finish cooking while the catfish steams atop them, taking in their flavors. A gremolata is a traditional condiment made of chopped herbs, garlic, and lemon zest. For an extra touch of flavor and tradition, add an anchovy to the gremolata.

Pasta helps round out this dish into a full meal. While a simple linguini is perfectly acceptable, this is a great dish for fluted or spiral-shaped pastas because their crevices will hold the sauce.

MAKES 4–6 SERVINGS

FOR THE GREMOLATA
- ¼ cup slivered almonds
- ¼ cup chopped oregano
- Zest of 1 lemon
- 3 garlic cloves, crushed
- ¼ teaspoon sea salt

FOR THE CATFISH
- 1 fennel bulb with fronds
- 3 leeks, white parts only
- 2 tablespoons extra-virgin olive oil
- Salt
- 3 medium ripe tomatoes, chopped
- ¾ cup pitted Kalamata olives, halved
- 4 small catfish fillets (about 1 pound)
- Freshly ground black pepper

TO SERVE
- 1 pound al dente pasta

To make the gremolata, in a small food processor, combine all ingredients. Pulse until a thick paste forms. Transfer the gremolata to a nonreactive bowl and allow it to rest for at least 30 minutes at room temperature for the best flavor development.

To make the fish, remove the fronds from the fennel bulb and reserve. Chop the bulb into ¼-inch pieces.

Clean the leeks by cutting them in half vertically and allowing them to float in a bowl of water cut-side down so that any grit in the bulbs will sink to the bottom of the bowl. Drain the leeks and cut into ¼-inch slices.

Heat the oil in a large skillet over medium heat. Add the fennel and leeks and a pinch of salt. Cook, stirring frequently, for 8–10 minutes, or until the fennel is softened. Add the tomatoes and olives and continue cooking for 10 minutes, or until the tomatoes release liquid and produce a heavy steam. Lay the fennel fronds over the vegetables in the skillet and arrange the catfish fillets on top. Season with salt and pepper to taste. Cover the skillet and continue cooking for 10–15 minutes, or until the thickest part of each fillet is white and flaky.

To serve, transfer the fillets to a dish and keep warm. Discard the fennel fronds. Stir the vegetables in the skillet, combining them well and mashing the tomatoes and fennel. Add the pasta and toss to coat with the sauce. Divide the pasta equally among 4–6 bowls. Top with the vegetable mixture. Top each bowl with a catfish fillet and a generous serving of gremolata.

Hungarian-Style Catfish Paprika with Sour Cream Noodles

Hungary is known for its paprika. After Christopher Columbus brought peppers back from the New World, they spread along the Mediterranean to Hungary, where a mild variety was eventually dried and ground up to make paprika. In 1937, Hungarian scientist Albert Szent-Györgyi won the Nobel Prize in Medicine for discovering vitamin C, using paprika, not oranges, in some of his experiments.

Hungary is less well known for catfish, but its rivers are full of our whiskered friends, including the giant specimens that fishermen love to talk about. This recipe is typical of the rich comfort food of Hungary.

MAKES 8 SERVINGS

FOR THE CATFISH

- ½ cup vegetable oil
- 2 pounds catfish fillets, cut into bite-sized pieces
- Salt
- 2 medium yellow onions, diced
- 2 medium green bell peppers, diced
- 2 medium tomatoes, chopped
- 1 tablespoon hot (or sharp) Hungarian paprika
- 1¾ cups sour cream
- 1 tablespoon all-purpose flour
- 2 tablespoons butter, cubed

FOR THE NOODLES

- 1 (12-ounce) package egg noodles
- 3–4 slices smoked bacon, finely diced
- 1½ cups sour cream, divided
- 1 (8-ounce) container small-curd cottage cheese
- Salt

TO SERVE
Sour cream
Italian parsley, chopped

To make the catfish, heat the oil in a large skillet over medium-high heat. Sprinkle the catfish with ½ teaspoon salt and, working in batches so as not to overcrowd the skillet, carefully cook the catfish until lightly browned and flaky, about 3 minutes. Place the fish on a paper towel–lined plate to drain.

Add the onions to the same oil used to cook the fish. Cook, stirring frequently, until the onions are light brown, about 15 minutes. Add the bell peppers, tomatoes, and paprika, stirring to combine. Continue cooking for 10 minutes, or until the bell peppers are soft and the tomatoes begin to break down.

In a small bowl, whisk together the sour cream and flour to combine well. Add the sour cream mixture to the onion mixture and stir gently to combine. Return the fish to the skillet, stirring gently to incorporate it without breaking it. Reduce the heat to low, cover the skillet, and simmer for 10 minutes. Add the butter one cube at a time, allowing each addition to melt into the sauce before adding the next. Season with salt to taste.

To make the noodles, preheat the oven to 350°.

Cook the noodles according to package directions. Drain the noodles and reserve.

Fry the bacon in a large oven-safe skillet over medium heat until crisp. Place the bacon bits on a paper towel–lined plate to drain, leaving as much of the drippings in the skillet as possible.

Reduce the heat to low and add 2 tablespoons of the sour cream to the bacon drippings in the skillet, stirring to combine. Add the reserved noodles and stir to coat them in the sour cream mixture. Spoon the remaining sour cream evenly over the top of the noodle mixture. Spread the cottage cheese over the noodles, sprinkle with the reserved bacon, and add salt to taste. Bake for 10 minutes, or until the cottage cheese has softened.

Serve the catfish on a bed of noodles topped with a dollop of sour cream and parsley.

Moroccan Catfish Tagine
Tajin bi'l-Hut

A tagine is a North African earthenware pot with a round bowl base and a conical cover. The cover allows condensation to return to the pot as a meal cooks in the base, making tagines ideal for braising tough meats. You don't need to have a special pot to make this, though. Tagine *also means any dish cooked in the pot, and this recipe focuses on the flavors found in a fish tagine, especially the traditional chermoula marinade.*

This dish traditionally uses catfish steaks. If you prefer not to deal with bones, substitute 3 thick catfish fillets. Cut the fillets in half lengthwise and arrange the pieces like pizza slices when you place them in the pot.

Plan ahead when making this recipe. The chermoula needs to rest for 1 hour to allow its flavors to develop, and then you'll need to allow an additional 2 hours of marinating time for the fish. But you don't have to worry about side dishes; this is truly a one-pot meal.

MAKES 6 SERVINGS

FOR THE CHERMOULA
- 6 tablespoons extra-virgin olive oil
- 6 garlic cloves, minced
- 1 shallot, minced
- ½ cup finely chopped cilantro
- ½ cup finely chopped Italian parsley
- Juice of ½ lemon
- 1 teaspoon hot paprika
- ½ teaspoon cumin
- ¼ teaspoon cinnamon
- ¼ teaspoon sumac
- 1¼ teaspoons salt
- 1 teaspoon freshly ground black pepper
- ¼ teaspoon cayenne pepper

FOR THE STEW

6 medium catfish steaks (about 1½ pounds)
1 tablespoon extra-virgin olive oil
2 medium red potatoes, peeled and sliced ⅛ inch thick
2 medium carrots, sliced ⅛ inch thick
1 small rutabaga, sliced ⅛ inch thick
Salt and freshly ground black pepper
1 green bell pepper, cut into thin strips
1 medium yellow onion, thinly sliced
2 large ripe tomatoes, peeled and thinly sliced
1 (8-ounce) can tomato sauce
2 tablespoons chopped cilantro
2 tablespoons chopped Italian parsley

To make the chermoula, mix all ingredients together in a medium bowl, cover, and refrigerate for at least 1 hour before using.

To make the stew, coat the catfish steaks with half of the chermoula and marinate them in a covered shallow baking dish in the refrigerator for 2 hours.

Preheat the oven to 400°.

Oil a tagine, Dutch oven, or covered casserole with the olive oil and arrange the potatoes, carrots, and rutabaga on the bottom. Season with salt and pepper. Lay the catfish steaks on top of the vegetables. Cover the fish with the bell pepper, onion, and tomatoes. Season again with salt and pepper.

Spoon half of the remaining chermoula over the tomatoes. Top the chermoula with the tomato sauce, sprinkle with the cilantro and parsley, and add more salt and pepper. Spoon the rest of the chermoula over everything.

Cover and bake for 1 hour, or until the fish is cooked through and the root vegetables are tender.

Catfish and Vegetable Tempura

Japanese food is now wildly popular across the South, particularly sushi. Initially this wasn't the case, however. The Japanese dishes that opened the door were teriyaki, the exotic but still recognizable grilled meat in a sweet sauce, and tempura, a natural for southerners since it's deep-fried. Tempura is a popular street food in Japan, usually featuring fish or shrimp along with vegetables. Though catfish isn't traditional, its sweetness and firmness make it ideal for tempura.

MAKES 4 SERVINGS

FOR THE TEMPURA BATTER
2 eggs, beaten
2 cups ice-cold water
2 cups flour
Cayenne pepper to taste
Salt and freshly ground black pepper to taste

FOR THE VEGETABLES AND CATFISH
1 head of broccoli, cut into florets
1 large sweet potato, peeled and cut into 1/4-inch slices
1 medium zucchini, cut into 1/4-inch slices
4 catfish fillets, cut into long strips

TO SERVE
Teriyaki, ponzu, or soy sauce for dipping
Steamed rice

Heat at least 3 inches of vegetable or peanut oil to 375° in a deep pot or deep fryer.

To make the tempura batter, in a large bowl, combine all ingredients to form a thin batter.

To prepare the vegetables, bring a large pot of water to a boil over high heat. Fill 2 large bowls with ice water, leaving enough room to hold the vegetables without overflowing. Add the broccoli to the boiling water. Cook for 2 minutes, or until the broccoli is bright green. Immediately transfer the broccoli to a bowl of ice water to stop the cooking process. Strain the broccoli.

Using the same pot of boiling water, cook the sweet potatoes for 5 minutes. Transfer the sweet potatoes to the other bowl of ice water and strain.

To make the tempura, dip the zucchini in the batter, making sure it's well coated. Shake off any excess batter.

Working in batches, place the zucchini carefully into the hot oil and cook for 1–2 minutes, or until the zucchini is a light golden brown. Place on a wire rack set over a baking sheet to drain. Allow the oil to return to 375° before starting the next batch. Follow the same procedure for the broccoli, except cook for 2–3 minutes. For the sweet potatoes, increase the cooking time to 3–4 minutes.

For the fish, dip the pieces into the batter, making sure the fish is totally coated. Gently shake off any excess batter. Working in small batches, no more than about 4 pieces at a time, place the fish carefully into the hot oil and cook for 4–6 minutes, or until golden brown.

Serve immediately with teriyaki, ponzu, or soy sauce for dipping and steamed rice.

NOTE ❋ Feel free to use other vegetables if the ones listed aren't to your liking. Cauliflower, onions, and mushrooms work well with this technique.

Miso-Marinated Catfish

Miso, fermented soybean paste, has been eaten in Japan since the Neolithic era. The white miso paste we use here, shiromiso, was first developed during Japan's illustrious Edo period. The mildest miso paste, it's a blend of rice and barley with only a small portion of fermented soybeans added to the mix.

We enhance the sweetness of the white miso by combining it with sake, a Japanese wine made from fermented rice, and mirin, a lower-alcohol sweet rice wine. Marinating the fish overnight allows the complex flavors of the miso to soak deeply into the fish. A quick sear in the skillet caramelizes the sugars in the marinade, then the fish finishes cooking in the oven.

Serve the fish with steamed rice and lightly sautéed greens or with a variety of Japanese pickles. In summer, coat corn on the cob with white miso paste, wrap it in foil, and grill it to serve with the fish.

MAKES 4 SERVINGS

FOR THE MARINADE
- 6 tablespoons white miso paste
- ¼ cup sake
- ¼ cup mirin
- 3 tablespoons raw sugar

FOR THE CATFISH
- 4 catfish fillets
- 2 tablespoons soy or peanut oil

To make the marinade, combine all ingredients in a small saucepan over medium-low heat, stirring just until the miso paste and sugar are dissolved.

Place the fish in a single layer in a nonreactive sealable container. Pour the marinade over the fish, seal, and refrigerate overnight or for up to 24 hours.

Preheat the oven to 400°.

Heat the oil in a medium heavy oven-safe skillet over medium-high heat. Working in batches to prevent crowding, sear each fillet until the surface is brown on both sides. Arrange all of the fillets in the skillet and bake for 10–15 minutes.

Caramelized Clay Pot Catfish
Cà Kho Tô

The clay pots used in traditional Vietnamese cooking are submerged in water prior to cooking so the water can be released as steam in the oven to keep the food moist. On the stovetop, the absorbed water keeps the clay from cracking due to the intense heat of the burner.

You're probably skeptical about the combination of caramel and catfish in this dish, but trust us on this. It works. This is a classic Vietnamese technique, and the sweetness of the caramel is tempered by the pungency of the garlic, shallots, and fish sauce. The burnt-sugar flavor adds an intriguing and unexpected depth to the dish. Serve the catfish with something simple like rice to let the flavors take you somewhere exotic.

MAKES 2–4 SERVINGS

3 tablespoons peanut or vegetable oil
3 shallots, diced
2 garlic cloves, minced
⅓ cup sugar
1 pound catfish steaks
2 tablespoons fish sauce
¼ teaspoon salt

TO SERVE
Cooked white rice
1 small red chili pepper, thinly sliced
2 green onions, diced
½ teaspoon freshly ground black pepper

SPECIAL EQUIPMENT
Asian clay pot (optional)

Heat the oil in a small saucepan over medium heat. Add the shallots and garlic and cook, stirring constantly, for 4 minutes, or until the garlic turns golden brown. Immediately strain the oil into a clay pot, stovetop-safe casserole, or small Dutch oven through a fine-mesh sieve. Discard the garlic and shallots.

Heat the flavored oil in the clay pot over medium-high heat. Add the sugar and 1 tablespoon water. Cook, stirring frequently, for 5 minutes, or until a dark caramel forms. Add the catfish steaks and turn to coat in the caramel. Add the fish sauce, salt, and 3 tablespoons water, stirring gently to combine. Bring the dish to a boil, cover, and reduce the heat to a simmer. Continue cooking for 5 minutes.

Serve over rice and garnish with the chili pepper, green onions, and pepper.

Thai Green Catfish Curry
Gang Kiew Wan Pla-dook

The word curry *can be confusing because it's used for so many things. It's derived from the Tamil word* kari, *meaning sauce. Curry powder was introduced to the West in the 1800s by British colonists in India. The leaves of the curry tree are included in some powders but not all. In Thailand, the source of inspiration for this recipe, curry blends are pastes rather than powders.*

Although the green curry paste here requires a large number of ingredients, it's easy to make. Just freeze the extra curry paste in ¼ cup batches and thaw a batch whenever you're in the mood. You can use the paste with other meats or for a vegetable curry. Galangal and shrimp paste can be found in most Asian markets.

MAKES 4 SERVINGS

FOR THE GREEN CURRY PASTE
- 1 stalk lemongrass (lower 2 inches), thinly sliced
- 1 (1-inch) piece galangal, thinly sliced
- 3 garlic cloves, minced
- 1 (½-inch) piece ginger, thinly sliced
- 1 shallot, sliced
- 2 green Thai chili peppers, sliced
- ½ cup chopped cilantro
- ½ cup minced basil
- 1 teaspoon shrimp paste
- 3 tablespoons fish sauce
- 3 tablespoons coconut milk
- 2 tablespoons lime juice
- 2 teaspoons lime zest
- 1 teaspoon light brown sugar
- ½ teaspoon cumin
- ½ teaspoon coriander
- ¼ teaspoon turmeric
- ½ teaspoon white pepper

Pinch of nutmeg
Salt to taste

FOR THE FISH
3 tablespoons vegetable oil, divided
8 small Thai or Indian eggplants, quartered
¼ cup green curry paste
1⅓ cups coconut milk, divided
1 pound catfish fillets, sliced crosswise into 4 pieces each
2 tablespoons fish sauce
1½ teaspoons dark brown sugar

TO SERVE
Cooked white rice
2 red Thai chili peppers, sliced diagonally
¼ cup Thai basil leaves

To make the curry paste, combine all ingredients in a food processor and pulse until a semismooth paste forms.

To make the dish, heat 2 tablespoons of the oil in a large skillet over medium heat and add the eggplants. Cook, stirring frequently, for 6–8 minutes, or until the eggplants are lightly browned on all sides and begin to soften. Transfer the eggplants to a bowl.

Heat the remaining 1 tablespoon oil in the same skillet over medium heat and add the curry paste. Cook, stirring constantly, for 5 minutes. Add ¼ of the coconut milk and cook, stirring frequently, until the curry paste is dissolved. Allow the mixture to simmer gently until a thin layer of oil rises to the top. Add the remaining coconut milk and let the mixture continue to simmer until the oil separates a second time. Add the reserved eggplants and cook for 10 minutes. Add the catfish, fish sauce, and brown sugar and continue to simmer until the catfish is tender, about 10 minutes.

Serve over rice and garnish with the chili peppers and basil.

Catfish 61

Chicken 65 is a popular dish in Chennai in the state of Tamil Nadu in southern India. This recipe is inspired by the name, not the dish, and U.S. Highway 61 through the Mississippi Delta.

Much of the nation's catfish comes from farms in the Delta, most of them not far off Highway 61. The flavors in this dish were influenced by the large number of Chinese immigrants to the Delta. Encouraged to come to the Delta to work as farm laborers in the late 1800s, Chinese Americans preferred to work for themselves and became owners of laundries and grocery stores. Through the grocery stores, they began to introduce Chinese food to the Delta. This recipe combines ingredients and techniques from both worlds.

The sauce is based on the flavors of Hoover Lee's famous Hoover Sauce. Mr. Lee sells this salty sweet sauce with a touch of heat at the Lee Hong Company grocery store in Louise, Mississippi. In our version, we use sorghum syrup to give the sauce a hint of the mystery that Mr. Lee infuses into each batch he prepares.

MAKES 4–6 SERVINGS

FOR THE SAUCE

4 tablespoons sorghum syrup
4 tablespoons soy sauce
1 tablespoon sriracha
1 tablespoon rice vinegar

FOR THE FISH

4 small catfish fillets (about 1 pound)
½ teaspoon white pepper
¼ teaspoon salt
6 medium tomatillos, husked and quartered
2 medium tomatoes, diced
8 ounces firm tofu, cubed
1 (½-inch) piece ginger, minced
2 tablespoons peanut or soy oil

2 garlic cloves, minced
4 slices bacon, chopped
8 pickled okra spears, quartered lengthwise

TO SERVE

Cooked white rice
2 green onions, thinly sliced
¼ cup chopped cilantro

To make the sauce, combine all ingredients in a small bowl, whisking until well incorporated.

To make the fish, sprinkle white pepper and salt on both sides of the fillets and place them in the bottom of a 3-quart casserole. Arrange the tomatillos, tomatoes, and tofu around the fish and sprinkle the ginger over it.

Heat the oil in a small skillet over medium heat. Add the garlic and cook, stirring constantly, until fragrant, about 2 minutes. Add the bacon and continue cooking, stirring constantly, until it just begins to crisp, about 8 minutes. Add the okra and cook, stirring constantly, for 1 minute. Add the sauce and bring to a boil, stirring frequently.

Remove the bacon and okra and scatter them over the fish fillets in the casserole. Pour the sauce over the fish and cover the casserole immediately. Transfer the casserole to a burner over medium heat and cook for 15 minutes, or until the fish is cooked through.

Serve over rice and garnish with the green onions and cilantro.

Nashville-Style Hot Fried Catfish

Nashville is home to an interesting phenomenon—hot chicken, or, as we like to think of it, masochism via food. The most widely accepted origin story revolves around Prince's Hot Chicken. According to family lore, one of the original owners was a womanizer who came home late one time too many. To punish him, his lady friend whipped up a batch of extra-hot chicken. Unfortunately for her but fortuitously for him, he actually liked the hot chicken and revenge resulted in a business plan. Ultimately the chicken became legendary and Prince's was named an American classic by the James Beard Foundation in 2013.

We've applied the technique to catfish, and the addictive endorphin rush remains. Prince's offers four levels of heat. To add more fire to this recipe, you can boost the amount of habanero hot sauce, add cayenne pepper to the breading, or slather on a thicker coating of dressing. You could even go crazy and make the dressing with hot chili oil instead of vegetable oil. Part of the magic is that the fish soaks in the buttermilk bath for at least 24 hours before cooking.

We would be remiss if we didn't warn you about the dangers of this recipe. Don't handle the marinade or the dressing with your bare hands. When eating the dish, don't use your hands, and if you touch your mouth with your hands, be sure not to get them near your eyes.

MAKES 6 SERVINGS

FOR THE MARINADE
½ cup buttermilk
⅓ cup habanero hot sauce

FOR THE CATFISH
3 pounds small catfish fillets

FOR THE BREADING
2 cups all-purpose flour
¾ teaspoon onion powder
2 teaspoons salt
¾ teaspoon freshly ground black pepper

FOR THE DRESSING
¼ cup vegetable oil
2 tablespoons apple cider vinegar
¼ teaspoon garlic powder
¼ teaspoon salt
3 tablespoons cayenne pepper
Pinch of sugar

TO SERVE
Dill pickles
Fresh slices of white bread

To make the marinade, combine the buttermilk and hot sauce in a large nonreactive sealable container. Add the catfish fillets, seal the container, and refrigerate for 24 hours.

To cook the fish, heat at least 3 inches of soy or peanut oil to 325° in a deep pot or deep fryer. Turn on an oven vent or open a window.

To make the breading, whisk together all ingredients in a large, shallow bowl. Remove the fillets from the buttermilk mixture and, using tongs, dredge each fillet in the seasoned flour, shaking off any excess.

Fry the fillets in batches for 3–4 minutes, or until golden brown. Drain the fish on a wire rack placed over paper towels.

To make the dressing, whisk together all ingredients.

To serve, brush the fried fillets with the dressing and plate them with dill pickles and slices of white bread.

Noodled Catfish Casserole

Tuna noodle casserole is enshrined in the pantheon of American food primarily because there's no moderate reaction to it. You either love it or hate it. For the record, Angela doesn't love it.

This dish is a nod to the sport of noodling catfish. Noodling catfish is performed by jumping into a lake or river, reaching into holes in the bank or under tree roots or fallen logs, and grabbing the catfish lurking there. The bait? The fisherman's thumb. When cornered, catfish will defend themselves by biting. Once bitten, all the fisherman has to do is hold on and haul out his prize.

We've never noodled ourselves, but we felt that the level of, um, dedication involved in noodling deserved recognition—hence this dish. We also couldn't pass up the opportunity to create a dish named Noodled Catfish Casserole. The best part is that it's delicious. The sweetness of catfish is one factor, but it's the mushrooms, manchego cheese, and hint of sherry that put the dish over the top.

MAKES 8 SERVINGS

- ½ pound curly egg noodles
- 1 cup dried shiitake mushrooms
- 1 cup boiling water
- 10 tablespoons butter, divided
- 2 stalks celery, diced
- 1 medium yellow onion, diced
- 6 tablespoons all-purpose flour
- 4 cups whole milk
- ¼ cup dry sherry
- 1 teaspoon fresh thyme leaves
- Salt
- 4 ounces Manchego cheese, grated
- Freshly ground black pepper
- 1 pound catfish fillets, diced

1½ cups panko breadcrumbs
¾ cup slivered almonds
1 tablespoon chopped parsley

Preheat the oven to 375°. Grease a 9 × 13-inch baking dish.

Cook the noodles al dente according to package directions. Rinse them under cold water and return them to the pot off the heat.

In a small bowl, soak the mushrooms in the boiling water for 10 minutes, using a smaller bowl to submerge them in the liquid. Drain the mushrooms, reserving the liquid. Finely chop the mushrooms. Strain the liquid through a fine-mesh sieve and reserve.

Melt 2 tablespoons of the butter in a medium saucepan over medium heat. Add the celery and onion and cook, stirring constantly, until the vegetables are soft, about 7 minutes. Add the vegetables to the pot with the noodles.

Return the saucepan to the stove and melt 4 tablespoons of the butter over medium-low heat. Add the flour and cook, stirring constantly, for 1 minute, or until the mixture is bubbly and light beige.

Increase the heat to medium. Whisking constantly, slowly add the milk, then the reserved liquid from the mushrooms, the sherry, the thyme, and 2½ teaspoons salt. Bring the mixture to a boil, whisking frequently to prevent sticking. Stir in the mushrooms and reduce the heat to low. Simmer the sauce for 2 minutes, or until it's thick enough to coat the back of a spoon. Add the cheese 1 ounce at a time, stirring until the cheese is melted before adding the next ounce.

Pour the sauce over the noodles and stir well. Season with salt and pepper to taste. Gently fold in the catfish.

In a food processor or blender, combine the remaining 4 tablespoons butter, cut into small pieces; the panko; the almonds; the parsley; ½ teaspoon salt; and ½ teaspoon pepper. Pulse to combine into a loose mixture.

Gently transfer the noodle mixture to the prepared baking dish and top it with the panko mixture. Bake the casserole for 25–30 minutes, or until the sauce is bubbly and the top is brown and crisp. Allow the casserole to rest for 5 minutes before serving.

Beer-Battered Catfish and Chips

Had the colonies not won the Revolutionary War, we have no doubt that today there would be pubs throughout the South serving catfish and chips. We're not saying that winning the war was a bad thing, but it's unfortunate that we were delayed from enjoying this great dish for a while because of it.

Fans of cornmeal-breaded fried catfish are very likely to enjoy this version as well. The beer keeps the batter light and adds flavor, and the thicker batter holds the black pepper kick. The batter is also very good for onion rings. Just cut an onion into ½-inch-thick slices. Separate the slices into rings and dredge the rings individually in the batter. Shake off any excess batter and fry the rings at 325° for 1–2 minutes, or until the batter is golden brown and crisp.

MAKES 6 SERVINGS

FOR THE CHIPS
4 large baking potatoes
Salt

FOR THE FISH
1½ cups all-purpose flour
1½ teaspoons salt
¼ teaspoon freshly ground black pepper
1 (12-ounce) can or bottle of beer
1 egg
2 pounds catfish fillets

TO SERVE
Malt vinegar
Tartar sauce

To make the chips, preheat the oven to 200°.

Heat at least 3 inches of soy or peanut oil to 325° in a deep pot or deep fryer.

Peel the potatoes and cut them into 1-inch-wide by ¼-inch-thick slices. Place the slices in a large bowl and cover them with water. Swirl the slices around with your hands until the water becomes cloudy to remove the excess starch. Drain the water from the potatoes, lay them out on paper towels, and pat dry.

Line one paper bag per fryer batch with paper towels.

Working in batches, transfer the potato slices to the hot oil and cook for 5–6 minutes. Transfer the semicooked potatoes to a prepared paper bag. Allow the oil to reheat to 325° before cooking the next batch.

When all of the potato slices have been semicooked, increase the oil temperature to 375°. Place a wire rack over a baking sheet.

Working in batches, transfer the potatoes to the hot oil and cook for 2–3 minutes, or until the chips are golden brown. Transfer them to the prepared baking sheet to drain any excess oil. Season with salt to taste. Allow the oil to return to 375° before cooking the next batch.

Place the baking sheet in the oven to keep the chips warm while preparing the fish.

To make the fish, return the oil to 375°.

In a large bowl, combine the flour, salt, and pepper, whisking to distribute the seasonings evenly through the flour. Slowly pour in the beer, whisking until a thick batter forms. Add the egg, whisking to combine thoroughly.

Cut the catfish fillets into quarters by slicing them in half lengthwise, then in half from top to bottom. Dip the catfish pieces into the batter, making sure to coat them completely. Allow any excess to drip off.

Working in batches, carefully lower the battered pieces into the hot oil and cook for 4–5 minutes, or until golden brown. Place the cooked pieces on a paper towel–lined plate to drain. Allow the oil to return to 375° before cooking more fish.

Serve the fish and chips with malt vinegar for drizzling and tartar sauce for dipping.

Catfish Pudding

Fear not—we wouldn't create a catfish dessert. We promise. Instead, this is a tribute to one of our favorite culinary destinations—the Lenten Waffle Shop at Calvary Episcopal Church in downtown Memphis. In 1928, Rosalie Rhett began serving waffles to the men who attended the daily Lenten services at the church. Today, the menu has expanded to include other dishes such as tomato aspic, spaghetti, chicken salad, and chicken hash, which is served with the waffles. We get excited about Mardi Gras because Mardi Gras leads to Lent and Lent leads to the Waffle Shop.

Perhaps the most beloved and misunderstood dish offered at the Waffle Shop is the oddly named fish pudding. At Calvary, fish pudding is a rich casserole or gratin made with cod. This recipe replaces the cod with catfish, but otherwise it's true to the recipe that has been served and enjoyed for over eighty years.

MAKES 6–8 SERVINGS

- 1 pound 10 ounces catfish fillets
- ½ cup plus 3 tablespoons cracker crumbs, divided
- 1⅓ cups milk
- 2½ tablespoons butter, melted
- ¼ cup chopped parsley
- 2 tablespoons grated white onions
- 2 tablespoons plus 2 teaspoons lemon juice
- 1 tablespoon dry sherry
- ¼ teaspoon baking soda
- Dash of Tabasco sauce
- 4 eggs, well beaten
- 2 tablespoons butter, cut into small cubes

Bring a large saucepan of lightly salted water to a boil over medium heat. Add the catfish and cook for 10 minutes, or until the fish is white and flakes easily. Drain the fish and place it on a paper towel–lined plate to absorb any excess water.

Preheat the oven to 450°. Butter a 2-quart baking dish.

In a large bowl, flake the fish with a fork, picking through to remove any bones. Stir in 3 tablespoons of the cracker crumbs and the milk, melted butter, parsley, onions, lemon juice, sherry, baking soda, and Tabasco sauce. Stir in the eggs.

Pour the pudding into the prepared dish and smooth the top with a spatula or spoon. Sprinkle the top evenly with the remaining ½ cup cracker crumbs and dot with the cubed butter.

Bake the pudding for 10 minutes. Reduce the oven temperature to 350° and continue baking for 20–30 minutes, or until the pudding is set.

Cross-Eyed Catfish with Wavy Gravy

Catfish plays a large role in American culture, especially in popular music. In bluesman Jimmy Rogers's song "My Last Meal," a condemned man is told that it's time for his last meal but that he won't be taken away until he gets what he asks for. Naturally, the man provides a rather challenging list, including dinosaur eggs and rattlesnake hips. The line that really caught our attention was a request for "two cross-eyed catfish an' some wavy gravy in a left-hand dish."

First, we thought about the Cross-Eyed Pig, a barbecue joint in Little Rock with a great rub. We decided to rub our catfish until they're cross-eyed. Of course wavy gravy brought to mind Hugh Romney, the hippie philosopher and peace activist of Woodstock fame. It was after Woodstock, at the Texas Pop Festival, that B. B. King gave Romney the name Wavy Gravy. Gravy's work at Woodstock inspired the rest of this dish.

At Woodstock, the task of feeding the massive crowds fell to Gravy and other members of the Hog Farm commune. Since they only had a small budget to feed the huge crowd, brown rice and any available vegetables became the staples of the food line. So here's a southern dish with a hippie twist.

MAKES 4 SERVINGS

FOR THE GRAVIES
1 pound beets, tops removed
Extra-virgin olive oil
1½ pounds zucchini
Salt
6 mint leaves, chopped
¼ teaspoon sugar
1 cup plain Greek yogurt
2 teaspoons horseradish
Juice of 1 lemon
¼ teaspoon lemon zest

FOR THE CATFISH
1 cup brown rice flour
2 teaspoons paprika
2 teaspoons dark brown sugar
1 teaspoon chili powder
½ teaspoon garlic powder
½ teaspoon cinnamon
1 teaspoon salt
½ teaspoon freshly ground black pepper
Pinch of cayenne pepper
4 catfish fillets (about 1 pound)

TO SERVE
4 lemon slices

SPECIAL EQUIPMENT
Left-hand dish (optional)

To make the gravies, preheat the oven to 400°.

Clean the beets thoroughly and place them in a baking dish. Lightly coat the beets on all sides with 1 tablespoon olive oil. Cover the pan with foil.

Remove the stems from the zucchini and cut the squash into 2-inch slices. Place the squash in a baking dish and toss them with 2 teaspoons olive oil and a pinch of salt.

Place both baking dishes in the oven. Bake the zucchini for 45 minutes, or until it's soft and collapsed. Bake the beets for 1½ hours. Remove the zucchini and beets from the oven when they're done and discard the foil over the beets. Allow the vegetables to cool enough to be handled.

Transfer the zucchini to a food processor and combine it with the mint, sugar, 1 teaspoon olive oil, and ¾ teaspoon salt. Pulse until a smooth purée forms. Place the zucchini purée in a small saucepan and cover to keep warm. Clean the food processor to use for the beets.

Peel the beets, then cube them. Transfer them to the food processor and add ½ teaspoon salt and the yogurt, horseradish, lemon juice, and lemon zest. Pulse until a smooth purée forms. Transfer the beet purée to a small saucepan and cover to keep warm while the fish cooks.

To make the fish, heat at least 3 inches of peanut or soy oil to 375° in a deep pot or deep fryer.

In a large bowl, combine the brown rice flour, paprika, brown sugar, chili powder, garlic powder, cinnamon, salt, black pepper, and cayenne pepper. Whisk to distribute the spices evenly through the flour.

Dredge each fillet in the brown rice flour mixture, coating it evenly on both sides.

Fry the fillets for 4–5 minutes, or until golden brown. Transfer the fillets to a wire rack placed over a baking sheet to drain.

To serve, decorate each plate with a wave of zucchini purée on one side and a wave of beet purée on the other, leaving enough room for a catfish fillet between the waves. Place a fillet between the waves and top it with a slice of lemon.

Acknowledgments

Thanks to everyone who has ever dropped a baited hook in the water or scooped out a net full of fish or lowered a basket of fish into hot oil. You have given us happy memories and full bellies all our lives.

Our friend Minter Byrd stepped up big time and led our outside testing efforts.

Our agent, Lisa Ekus, has been not only an excellent guide but a wonderful friend as well.

And as always, all the folks at the University of North Carolina Press are amazing and a joy to work with.

Index

Appetizers
  Catfish and Bacon Brochettes, 36
  Catfish Croquetas, 40
  Catfish Empanadas, 42
  Catfish Fritters, 50
  Catfish with Baba Ghanoush, 38
  Coriander Catfish Rolls, 48
  Dodson Lake Samosas, 45
  Mississippi Bao, 51
  Smoky Catfish Brandade Spread, 56
  Smoky Catfish Mousse, 54
  Tea-Smoked Catfish, 58

Baked Catfish with Citrus, 92
Beer-Battered Catfish and Chips, 129
Blackened Catfish, 98
Butter-Poached-Catfish Surf and Turf, 94

Cajun Cabbage, 33
Caramelized Clay Pot Catfish, 118
Catfish: buying, 11; cuts of, 12–13; deep-frying, 13–15
Catfish and Bacon Brochettes, 36
Catfish and Vegetable Tempura, 114
Catfish *Bánh Mì*, 88
Catfish Burgers, 84
Catfish Chowder, 62
Catfish Croquetas, 40
Catfish Empanadas, 42
Catfish *en Papillote*, 104
Catfish Fritters 50
Catfish Gumbo, 64
Catfish Po'Boys, 82

Catfish Pudding, 132
Catfish-Rice Soup with Ginger and Onion, 66
Catfish Sauce Piquant, 74
Catfish 61, 122
Catfish Tacos, 86
Catfish with Baba Ghanoush, 38
Coleslaw 28
Colombian Catfish Pie, 102
Coriander Catfish Rolls, 48
Creamy Catfish-Pecan Salad, 78
Cross-Eyed Catfish with Wavy Gravy, 134

Delta Paella, 106
Dodson Lake Samosas, 45

Entrées
  Baked Catfish with Citrus, 92
  Beer-Battered Catfish and Chips, 129
  Blackened Catfish, 98
  Butter-Poached-Catfish Surf and Turf, 94
  Caramelized Clay Pot Catfish, 118
  Catfish and Vegetable Tempura, 114
  Catfish *en Papillote*, 104
  Catfish Pudding, 132
  Catfish 61, 122
  Colombian Catfish Pie, 102
  Cross-Eyed Catfish with Wavy Gravy, 134
  Delta Paella, 106
  Hungarian-Style Catfish Paprika with Sour Cream Noodles, 110
  Jerk Catfish, 100

Maple Planked Catfish, 96
Mediterranean-Style Steamed Catfish, 108
Miso-Marinated Catfish, 116
Moroccan Catfish Tagine, 112
Nashville-Style Hot Fried Catfish, 124
Noodled Catfish Casserole, 126
Thai Green Catfish Curry, 120

Fried catfish, 16
   Fried Catfish Fillets, 26
   Fried Catfish Steaks, 22
   Fried Whole Catfish, 20
   Popcorn Catfish, 24
   Thin-Fried Catfish, 18
Fried Catfish Fillets, 26
Fried Catfish Steaks, 22
Fried Whole Catfish, 20

Grilled Catfish Salad, 80

Hungarian-Style Catfish Paprika with Sour Cream Noodles, 110
Hushpuppies, 29

Indonesian Spicy-and-Sour Catfish Soup, 70

Jerk Catfish, 100

Maple Planked Catfish, 96
Mediterranean-Style Steamed Catfish, 108
Miso-Marinated Catfish, 116
Mississippi Bao 51
Moroccan Catfish Tagine, 112

Nashville-Style Hot Fried Catfish, 124
Nigerian Catfish Stew, 68
Noodled Catfish Casserole, 126

Pickled Green Tomatoes, 30
Popcorn Catfish, 24

Sauces
   Catfish Sauce Piquant, 74
   Tartar Sauce, 27
Salads
   Creamy Catfish-Pecan Salad, 78
   Grilled Catfish Salad, 80
Sandwiches
   Catfish *Bánh Mì*, 88
   Catfish Burgers, 84
   Catfish Po'Boys, 82
   Catfish Tacos, 86
Side dishes
   Cajun Cabbage, 33
   Coleslaw, 28
   Hushpuppies, 29
   Pickled Green Tomatoes, 30
   Smoky Catfish Brandade Spread, 56
   White Beans, 32
Smoky Catfish Mousse, 54
Soups and stews
   Catfish Chowder, 62
   Catfish Gumbo, 64
   Catfish-Rice Soup with Ginger and Onion, 66
   Indonesian Spicy-and-Sour Catfish Soup, 70
   Nigerian Catfish Stew, 68
   Szechuan Catfish Stew, 72
Szechuan Catfish Stew, 72

Tartar Sauce, 27
Tea-Smoked Catfish, 58
Thai Green Catfish Curry, 120
Thin-Fried Catfish, 18

White Beans, 32